Lost in a Labyrinth of Red Tape

LOST IN A
LABYRINTH OF
RED TAPE

The Story of an Immigration that Failed

ARMIN SCHMID AND RENATE SCHMID

With a Foreword by Wolfgang Benz
Translated by Margot Bettauer Dembo

NORTHWESTERN UNIVERSITY PRESS

Evanston, Illinois

Northwestern University Press
Evanston, Illinois 60208-4210

First published 1993 as *Im Labyrinth der Paragraphen: Die Geschichte einer gescheit-erten Emigration* by Fischer Taschenbuch Verlag, Frankfurt. Copyright © 1993 by Fischer Taschenbuch Verlag. English translation published 1996 by arrangement with Fischer Taschenbuch Verlag. Copyright © 1996 by Northwestern University Press. All rights reserved

Printed in the United States of America

ISBN CLOTH 0-8101-1185-3
ISBN PAPER 0-8101-1170-5

Library of Congress Cataloging-in-Publication Data

Schmid, Armin.
    [Im Labyrinth der Paragraphen. English]
    Lost in a labyrinth of red tape : the story of an immigration
that failed / Armin Schmid and Renate Schmid ; with a foreword by
Wolfgang Benz ; translated by Margot Bettauer Dembo.
    p. c. — (Jewish lives)
    ISBN 0-8101-1185-3 (cloth : alk. paper). — ISBN 0-8101-1170-5
(paper)
    1. Bader, Helga, 1920– . 2. Jews—Germany—Biography. 3.
Jews—Germany—History—1933–1945. 4. Germany—Ethnic relations.
I. Schmid, Renate. II. Title. III. Series.
DS135.G5B24713 1996
940.53'18'092—dc20
[B]   96-12378
                                                CIP

Contents

❧

Foreword

Fewer than half of all the German Jews, who were discriminated against, persecuted, and eventually murdered by the National Socialist regime, were able to save themselves by fleeing abroad. Why their number was not larger is a question that has often been asked. A partial answer is that the majority of German Jews, who had deep roots in German culture, could not imagine in 1933, 1935, or even 1937 the fate that lay in store for them. After Kristallnacht—the officially staged pogrom in November 1938—when the handwriting on the wall became clear, it was too late for many of them. By then the bureaucratic obstacles to emigration were so great that most of those who wanted to leave could no longer surmount them.

But it was not just the small annoyances and administrative procedures devised by the German authorities that made emigration into a dangerous all-or-nothing game—it was also the endless, wearisome waiting outside consular and shipping offices; running to the police station, to the tax bureau, to all kinds of other agencies; and the negotiations with the customs and the shipping officials that in the end often turned out to be in vain. Another problem, at least as difficult, was finding a country that would grant them asylum, if possible with reasonable conditions, before it was too late.

At the same time the Nazi state was forcing German Jews to leave the country, it also put a brake on emigration. Driving the Jews out of the economy was supposed to encourage them to emigrate, but seizing all they had through property confiscation and ruinous taxes checked emigration possibilities. No country is interested in impoverished immigrants, and one of the insidious aims of the Nazi regime was to export anti-Semitism along with the emigrating Jews, hoping that those who were driven out of Germany would become welfare problems in their host countries.

An international conference took place in July 1938 at Évian, a French resort town on Lake Geneva. Convened by President Roosevelt, the conference was to deal with the emigration of Jews from Germany. Representatives from thirty-two countries and many Jewish organizations attended. But aside from the establishment of an "Intergovernmental Committee for Refugees" with headquarters in London and the vague assurance by a few countries that their existing immigration quotas could be fully used in the future, nothing happened to improve Jewish chances to emigrate from lands under Hitler's control.

For many Jews, the U.S. immigration quotas were an insurmountable barrier. Yet these annual quotas were not even filled before 1939, primarily because of the foreign exchange controls in Germany and the restrictive policy of the American immigration authorities. True, after the November 1938 pogrom, restrictions were eased, but for many it was already too late. If at first there was concern in the United States about the prospect of being burdened by impoverished Jews from central Europe, once war broke out there was the added fear of Nazi spies who might infiltrate the country with the stream of refugees. In spite of that, the United States was the most sought-after destination, and more than 130,000 German and Austrian Jews found refuge there.

The story of the failed emigration of the Frühauf family from Meiningen—one of the many stories of futile attempts by Jews to flee from Germany—is recorded in the certificates, documents, letters, and emigration papers that survived the Nazi regime and the postwar turmoil in a suitcase in Berlin. Helga Frühauf got the suitcase back in May 1946. Years later, she made the documents available to Armin and Renate Schmid. In the course of many conversations with her they were able to reconstruct the story of a Jewish family, lost in a labyrinth of red tape, for whom the route to safety in the United States remained blocked. Helga died in Frankfurt on March 17, 1995. The documents relating to the Frühauf family's unsuccessful attempts to emigrate are now in the Jewish Museum in Frankfurt.

WOLFGANG BENZ

❧

Departure for the New World

As was the custom in those days, Hermann Schwerin, a Jewish journeyman butcher from Brilon in the Sauerland, took to the road. In 1886, filled with a sense of adventure and because he wanted to see the world, he crossed the ocean to seek his fortune in the New World, as so many other Germans were doing at that time.

In New York he met Lina Stern, a pert and attractive young woman from Stammheim in Hesse. As a headstrong sixteen-year-old, she had run off to America because she and her stepmother were constantly getting in each other's hair. Once in New York, Lina stayed with a cousin.

Hermann and Lina were married and opened a kosher butcher shop in the Bronx. Thanks to the large Jewish population in that borough, the business prospered.

On August 7, 1892, their daughter, Johanna, whom they called Hilde, was born, and on March 2, 1896, a son, Monroe, arrived. Theirs could have turned into a conventional immigrants' story, but things didn't work out that way. Hermann Schwerin could not cope with the New York climate, and when he became ill, his doctor recommended that he return to "the old country."

The Return to the Old Country

The family left the United States for Germany in 1897. Upon their arrival, Hermann Schwerin's sister and brother-in-law in Cologne took them in. Now a new livelihood had to be found. The brother-in-law, known as "Germany's Clothing King," was the owner of the firm Leopold Juda; he offered to help Hermann and Lina set up a ready-to-wear clothing store for men and boys in Lüdenscheid.

I

FIGURE 1. Successful businessman and cattle dealer Simon Frühauf and his wife, Therese, née Vomberg (photographed in 1884 in Meiningen). Their son Felix married Hilde Schwerin in 1919. Felix and Hilde's daughter, Helga (born in 1920), was the only member of the family to survive the Naxi period.

From the outset business was good. The young couple, with great enthusiasm and the proverbial German industriousness, built up their business, at first without hired help. After only two years they were able to move to quarters twice the size of the original store.

The Schwerins kept a middle-class Jewish home. Lina took on

Jewish girls to live with the family and help with the housework. One of these young women, Else Dokter from Meiningen, formed a close friendship with the Schwerins' daughter, Hilde. Even after Else returned to Meiningen and married, the two stayed in touch. One day Else informed Hilde, "I've got just the man for you!" This kind of matchmaking is rooted in Jewish tradition.

And so a meeting was arranged with the candidate, Felix Frühauf (born on October 2, 1886). It took place in Bad Kissingen, in accordance with all the rules of propriety, and under the watchful eyes of Hilde's aunt and uncle.

Hilde and Felix liked each other at first sight. In August 1919 they celebrated their engagement, and on December 29 of that year they were married. The couple had an auspicious start; right after their wedding trip, they were able to move into Felix's completely furnished house on Wettiner Strasse in Meiningen.

Felix had learned his trade in Meiningen, working as a wholesaler, and in 1915 he had established a wholesale leather-goods firm that supplied primarily the toy and doll industry. Later that year, when "his country called," Felix served as an infantryman until the end of World War I. He was awarded the Iron Cross 2nd Class and came home unscathed. His brother Max, however, was killed in battle.

Felix immediately went back to work, and since dolls were no longer being made of leather, he switched over to supplying the saddle, upholstery, and shoe trades. He successfully guided his firm through inflation and recession in spite of all the political and economic turbulence of those postwar years.

A Happy Childhood

On December 19, 1920, a daughter, Helga, was born to the Frühaufs, and on November 6, 1922, a son, Rudolf, joined the family. In 1927 Felix sold the old house and purchased a villa with a sizable plot of land at 18 Leipziger Strasse in one of the best residential sections of Meiningen—a sign of his growing affluence. For the children the large garden was like a paradise where they and their friends could romp and make noise to their hearts' content.

Helga and Rudolf's religious upbringing was very strict; going to

FIGURE 2. Helga's parents, Hilde Schwerin and Felix Frühauf, at the time of their engagement (photo postcard, 1919).

the synagogue every Friday evening and on Saturday was a faithfully observed ritual. Twice a week they attended Hebrew school, much to their dismay, for while they were there, the other children were having fun playing games. Sundays they visited their paternal grandparents in Walldorf—at first they walked, but later, with a great to-do, they pedaled there on new bicycles.

FIGURE 3. Helga Frühauf and her brother, Rudolf (photo postcard, 1931).

The Frühaufs were solid, respected people. They ran a comfortable home and saw themselves as good Germans of the Jewish faith eager to belong to the assimilated Jewish upper class. Hilde was active in the executive committee of the League of Jewish Women; Felix was vice president of the German Association of Jewish War Veterans and a member of the Central Association of German Citi-

zens of the Jewish Faith. Both Christian and Jewish friends frequently came to their home, enjoying the family's warm hospitality.

At that time Meiningen had some 20,000 inhabitants, among
them 320 Jews. The Jewish community stuck together, although
from time to time there were tensions between the German Nationalist Jews and the Zionists. Nevertheless, a polite distance was main-
tained between them. On the whole, Jews and Christians lived side
by side without problems. This was also apparent when Helga started public school in 1927. An entry in her mother's diary says explicit-
ly that the child was happy to go to school and was completely inte-
grated in her class. When she changed to the Lyceum (a girls'
secondary school emphasizing languages) in 1931, she of course also
had Christian girlfriends. In later years Helga spoke enthusiastically
about her happy childhood in her parents' warm and protective
home where the children were shielded from worries. Life was quite
carefree—until Hitler came to power.

❖

Storm Clouds

After the Nazis seized power on January 30, 1933, one of the prime elements of their political policy was the persecution of Jews. On April 1 a boycott of all businesses belonging to Jews was implemented, followed on April 7 by the dismissal of Jews from the civil service and the exclusion of all Jews from the practice of law, except for those who had been frontline soldiers.

In Meiningen the Nazis marked April 1 with a boycott of Jewish businesses, doctors, and lawyers. The SA and SS marched up and down in front of Jewish stores carrying placards reading "Don't buy from Jews"; they distributed anti-Semitic leaflets and prevented people from entering the offices of Jewish doctors and lawyers. Some Germans who disregarded the boycott were openly photographed.

"We didn't notice much of this," Helga recalled. The Frühauf wholesale firm, which was located in a rear courtyard, was spared. Only a splatter of fresh paint on the front door of their house announced, "A Jew lives here." Felix removed the paint, and with that the matter was closed.

Even though Meiningen's fanatic Nazis agitated against the Jews, the small-town milieu prevented greater excesses. People of all faiths had business and personal relationships and had "become intertwined." Precisely for that reason the Frühaufs sought to shield their children, and nothing further was said in the family about what had happened.

Many Jews believed that these ugly incidents were just temporary, that Hitler would not remain in power for long, and that eventually everything would turn out well. Felix Frühauf shared this view. He was a dedicated German Nationalist. Hadn't he fought in the Great War? Hadn't he been decorated with the Iron Cross? Surely he would be safe from discrimination. This conviction, which was widespread among German Jews, kept many from emigrating while there was still time. For the same reasons, Felix turned a deaf ear to the warning of his father-in-law, Hermann Schwerin, who shortly before his death in 1931 had urged his daughter, "Take your husband, your children, and your mother and go back where you were born: go to America."

On September 15, 1935, the "Nuremberg Laws" (including a law that denied Jews citizenship in the German Reich and a law "to protect German blood and German honor" that made intermarriage between Jews and "Aryans" and the employment of female Aryan servants by Jews illegal) went into effect. Nazi policies became ever more hostile in an attempt to drive a wedge between Aryans and Jews. Every sort of contact was to be avoided.

As a consequence, Jews were expelled from the sports clubs. The German Association of Jewish War Veterans in Meiningen reacted immediately and set up its own sports arena with the full support of the Jewish community. The interesting events that took place there and the positive popular response to them provoked a group of Nazis. One night they destroyed the Jewish sports facility. This riot served to strengthen the solidarity of the Jewish community, and efforts were immediately made to rebuild the arena. But the fanatic Jew haters also smashed the new facility and went on to celebrate their victory at a roadside tavern in Landsberg. On their way home, stewed to the gills, five of the men were riding in a car that hit a tree. All were killed. Still the Jews did not knuckle under; once again they rebuilt their sports facility. But in the long run, the continuing anti-Semitic rampages appreciably dampened their enthusiasm for sports.

Discrimination against Jewish Students

The impact of the restrictions on the admission of Jews to schools and the introduction of segregated classes was felt in Meiningen, too. All Jewish children were expelled from the upper schools, except the sons and daughters of Jewish war veterans who had been given free tuition. In those days that amounted to 200 marks for the first child, with succeeding siblings admitted free. A new law canceled this provision, and now parents had to pay for each child, a financial

Im Namen des Führers und Reichskanzlers

Dem

Kaufmann Felix P r ü h a u f

in M e i n i n g e n

ist auf Grund der Verordnung vom 13. Juli 1934 zur Erinnerung an den Weltkrieg 1914/1918 das von dem Reichspräsidenten Generalfeld= marschall von Hindenburg gestiftete

Ehrenkreuz für Frontkämpfer

verliehen worden.

Meiningen , den 24. Januar   1935 .

Landrat des Landkreises.

Nr.   P.   39/35.

FIGURE 4. Award certificate, "Ehrenkreuz für Frontkämpfer" (Cross of Honor for Front-line Soldiers), January 24, 1935. It is noteworthy that as late as 1935 Jewish frontline soldiers were still being decorated.

catastrophe for the less well-off. Then the number of Jewish students was further reduced, and only Jewish children of "fathers with wartime decorations" were still admitted to the schools.

Any Jewish students who were left back were instantly thrown out of school. Moreover, Nazi teachers manipulated the grades of Jewish students downward, so that these poor children received only 4s and 5s* for their work and flunked out. This fate also befell Helga Frühauf. Her teacher gave her a grade of 4 on a perfect paper because, he said, the numbers she had written were illegible.

In this dire situation, the head of the commercial high school, Dr. Kalbfleisch—a so-called half-Jew—took the Jewish children under his wing. Helga attended his school from 1935 until the fall of 1936. But then even Dr. Kalbfleisch could no longer protect his pupils from the sadists among his teachers, and in the end he himself had to resign.

Two teachers who were particularly faithful to the Nazi party line

---

*The marking system was numerical, 1 being the best grade and 5 the worst.

had banished the three Jewish students in Helga's class to the back seats in the classroom. In order to make the gulf between them and the Aryan students even more visible and to prevent any contact in keeping with the concept of "racial separation," three rows of benches between the two groups had to remain empty. Helga refused to endure these humiliations any longer. After some dramatic scenes at home, Helga's mother took her out of school in the fall of 1936.

But what kind of job could Helga now get without a high school diploma? Her mother had been a Red Cross nurse, caring for wounded soldiers for three years during the war. She had been awarded the Cross of Honor for her service, so she hoped that her daughter could become a children's nurse. But since Helga was not yet eighteen years old, she could not find employment in a children's home or sanatorium.

Barely Sixteen and Off to Berlin

A cousin of Helga's was a dressmaker in Berlin. Encouraged by her example, Helga decided she wanted to learn dressmaking, too, and in October 1936, prior to her sixteenth birthday, she left for the capital city. However, by then apprenticeship contracts with Jews had been prohibited, and a decree that forbade Jews to move from one town to another was an additional obstacle. In spite of that, her cousin's teacher took her in and trained her, under the pretense that she was live-in household help. During that time Helga's cousin left for America. After completing her first year of apprenticeship, Helga found a position with two Jewish women from Czechoslovakia who had a ready-to-wear dressmaking shop. It turned out to be a short interlude because three-quarters of a year later the women emigrated to England. Helga was able to stay with a dressmaking teacher and even attend a cutting school. On the last day of December 1938 all that came to an end with a decree that all Jewish tradespeople had to close their businesses and shops.

Despite these job woes, Helga Frühauf liked to recall her Berlin years. In the anonymity of the big city she was still able to move about freely. Above all she enjoyed the dynamic cultural life of Berlin's Jewish community. She found many friends in the dance classes given by Frieda Bernstein, who instructed her pupils not only in the art of dance but also in etiquette. The graduation balls in the luxurious rooms of the Jewish Brotherhood (*Brüderverein*) house or in the Hotel König were unforgettable. After dance class the young people met in Café Uhlands Eck, which had dancing, or in a Jewish ice cream parlor. Precisely because National Socialism excluded Jews from so many aspects of German life, they pursued their own cultural and social activities that much more. Affluent Jewish families held balls and garden parties in their villas and parks in Dahlem. Helga was invited to parties given by the Arnsbergs, Silbersteins, Landsbergs, Sommers, Deutsches, and Jaffees. She joined the Jewish Cultural Club (*Jüdischer Kulturbund*), which was founded in 1933. The best Jewish actors—who had been banned from appearing on German stages—performed there. She got to know famous artists such as Alfred Berliner, Wolfram Bernstein, Max Ehrlich, and Walter Herz. In addition to plays, operas, operettas, and concerts, there were lectures on a wide variety of subjects. The Cultural Club, as well as the Emigration Organization and the Palestine Agency, offered language courses as a preparation for emigrating. Helga took private English lessons.

Kristallnacht—*The Night of Shattered Glass: Helga's Father Is Taken to a Concentration Camp*

In 1938 anti-Semitism became ever more blatant. On April 26 a decree was issued requiring Jews to have all their domestic and foreign property and assets evaluated and registered. On July 23 they were forced to carry compulsory identity cards. On August 17 came the order that all Jews be given "characteristic" middle names like Sara and Israel. After October 5 all Jewish passports were marked with a *J*. The Nazi government collected 5 marks each time one of these alterations had to be made in documents and papers. Then, on the night of November 9–10, sheer terror broke out: *Kristallnacht!*

The incident that supposedly triggered what the Nazis called the "anger of the people against the Jews" was the murder of Ernst vom Rath, the secretary to the German legation in Paris, by Herschel Grynszpan, a Jew. In Berlin, as in all other German cities and towns,

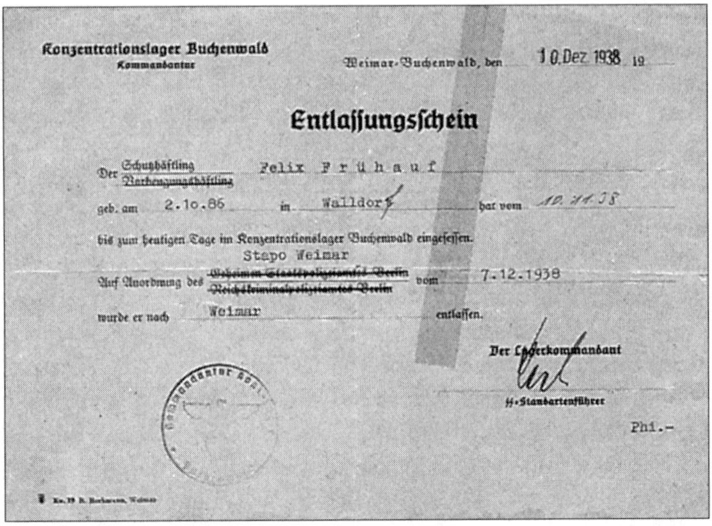

Konzentrationslager Buchenwald
Kommandantur

Weimar-Buchenwald, den 10.Dez 1938 19

Entlassungsschein

Der Schutzhäftling ~~Vorbeugungshäftling~~ Felix Frühauf

geb. am 2.10.86 in Walldorf hat vom 10.11.38

bis zum heutigen Tage im Konzentrationslager Buchenwald eingesessen.

Auf Anordnung des Stapo Weimar ~~Geheimen Staatspolizeiamtes Berlin~~ ~~Reichskriminalpolizeiamtes Berlin~~ vom 7.12.1938

wurde er nach Weimar entlassen.

Der Lagerkommandant

SS-Standartenführer

Phi.-

FIGURE 5A. Felix Frühauf's certificate of discharge from Buchenwald Concentration Camp on December 7, 1938. (The document is dated December 10, 1938.)

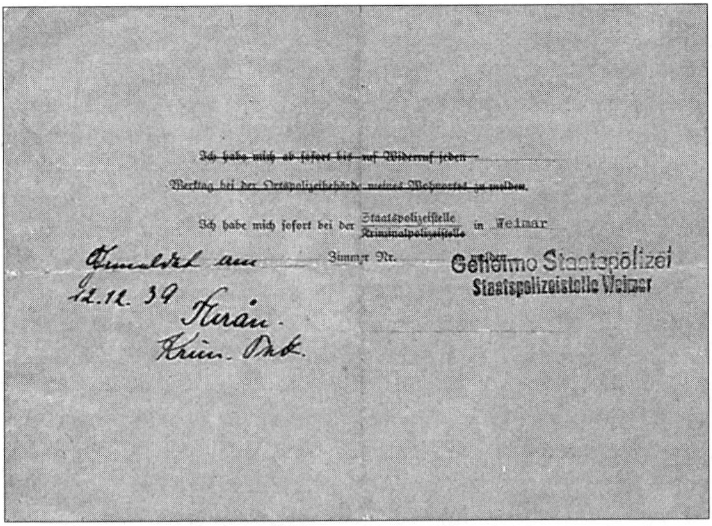

~~Ich habe mich ab sofort bis auf Widerruf jeden~~

~~Werktag bei der Ortspolizeibehörde meines Wohnortes zu melden.~~

Ich habe mich sofort bei der Staatspolizeistelle ~~Kriminalpolizeistelle~~ in Weimar

Zimmer Nr. melden.

Gemeldet am 12.12.39 Thrän. Krim. Ast.

Geheime Staatspolizei
Staatspolizeistelle Weimar

FIGURE 5B. Reverse side of the discharge certificate from Buchenwald Concentration Camp, with the handwritten date and signature of Officer Thrän indicating that Felix Frühauf had reported to the Gestapo office in Weimar on December 12, 1939.

FIGURE 6.
Passport photo of Felix Frühauf, 1938

synagogues were set on fire, Jewish stores and apartments were destroyed, Jewish pedestrians were beaten, and many men between the ages of seventeen and sixty-five were dragged off to concentration camps.

When Helga sensed that the wild rampages of the Nazi hordes were finally beginning to peter out, she ran downstairs and, passing agitated and distraught people in the streets, she headed for her aunt's house, utterly shocked by the destruction all around her.

Arriving at her aunt's place, the first thing she did was telephone her family in Meiningen. Her distraught mother told her that her father had been arrested. She was also in a panic because Helga's younger brother, Rudolf, had come rushing home from his job as an apprentice in Guben in Niederlausitz, even though his boss, Emanuel Meyer, had offered to emigrate to England with him. That would have been Rudolf's salvation. "For God's sake, Helga, stay in Berlin," her mother begged her. "You're safer there."

Hilde Frühauf spared no effort to obtain the release of her husband, who had been taken to the Buchenwald concentration camp, and for help she turned to Dr. Lederer, a lawyer in Gotha who was a family friend. So far the Nazis had not dared to touch him; after all, he was a Jewish war hero who had been awarded Germany's highest order, the Pour le Mérite. After four weeks Dr. Lederer succeeded in getting Felix out of the concentration camp.

Felix's wartime comrade-in-arms Thrän, now a police officer in Meiningen, also helped. He had already done what he could to secure Frühauf's release, and now he visited the ailing Felix almost daily, bringing him fruit and other things and assuring him: "Felix, believe me, I have tried to do everything possible for you! I'll always be there for you! If you need something, send for me. Only don't ever call me on the telephone!"

The Plunder of the Jews

The Kristallnacht pogrom was not enough to satisfy the Nazis. On November 12, 1938, they issued a decree demanding an "atonement payment" of one billion Reichsmarks—the so-called Grynszpan contribution. In addition, the Jews were to pay for repairing all damages the Nazis had caused. Insurance payments were confiscated and turned over to the Reich.

Notices outlining the levy on Jewish property were delivered to the Frühauf household on December 7. Hilde was required to pay 2,800 marks; Felix, who had petitioned the Nazi-appointed governor of Thüringen for a reduction, had to pay 2,200 marks. These amounts were to be paid in four installments by August 15, 1939. In addition, a further installment of 700 and 550 marks, respectively, was extorted in November from Felix and Hilde. It was to be paid within ten days.

Jewish Economic Life Is Destroyed

Jewish doctors and lawyers had been forbidden to practice their professions in June and September 1938, respectively, and on December 31, 1938, German Jews were completely excluded from the economic life of the country. The closing of all Jewish commercial enterprises was for the time being the most extensive persecution measure. This enormous governmentally organized thievery, which was called Aryanization, forced the Jews to sell their businesses at any price

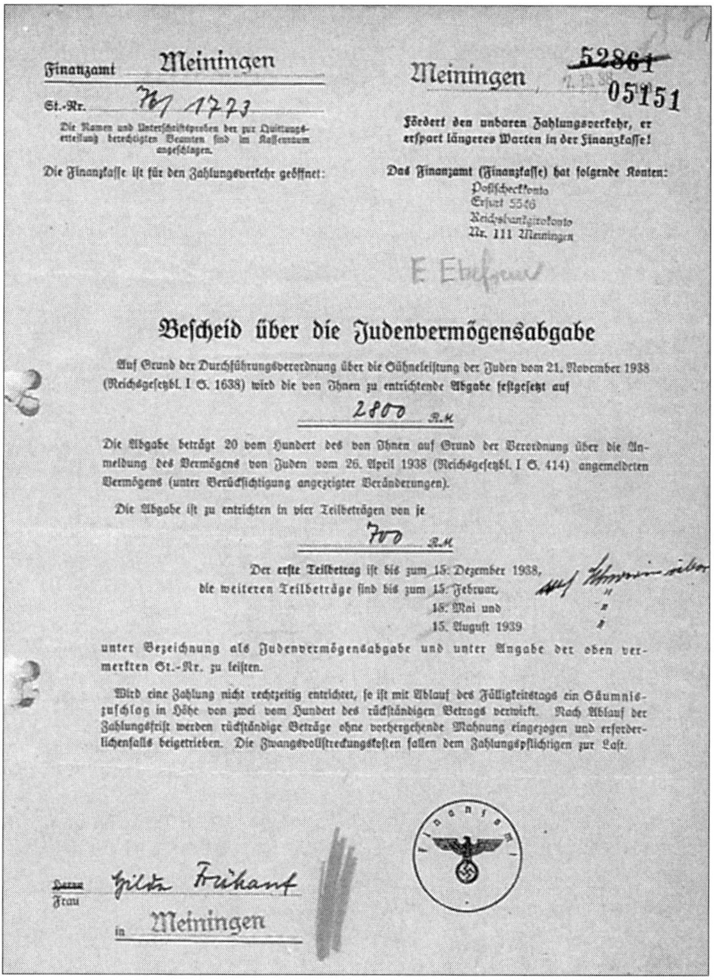

Finanzamt Meiningen

St.-Nr. 1773

Die Namen und Unterschriftsproben der zur Quittungserteilung berechtigten Beamten sind im Kassenraum angeschlagen.

Die Finanzkasse ist für den Zahlungsverkehr geöffnet:

Meiningen, 05151

Fördert den unbaren Zahlungsverkehr, er erspart längeres Warten in der Finanzkasse!

Das Finanzamt (Finanzkasse) hat folgende Konten:
Postscheckkonto
Erfurt 5546
Reichsbankgirokonto
Nr. 111 Meiningen

Bescheid über die Judenvermögensabgabe

Auf Grund der Durchführungsverordnung über die Sühneleistung der Juden vom 21. November 1938 (Reichsgesetzbl. I S. 1638) wird die von Ihnen zu entrichtende Abgabe festgesetzt auf

2800 RM

Die Abgabe beträgt 20 vom Hundert des von Ihnen auf Grund der Verordnung über die Anmeldung des Vermögens von Juden vom 26. April 1938 (Reichsgesetzbl. I S. 414) angemeldeten Vermögens (unter Berücksichtigung angezeigter Veränderungen).

Die Abgabe ist zu entrichten in vier Teilbeträgen von je

700 RM

Der erste Teilbetrag ist bis zum 15. Dezember 1938,
die weiteren Teilbeträge sind bis zum 15. Februar,
15. Mai und
15. August 1939

unter Bezeichnung als Judenvermögensabgabe und unter Angabe der oben vermerkten St.-Nr. zu leisten.

Wird eine Zahlung nicht rechtzeitig entrichtet, so ist mit Ablauf des Fälligkeitstags ein Säumniszuschlag in Höhe von zwei vom Hundert des rückständigen Betrags verwirkt. Nach Ablauf der Zahlungsfrist werden rückständige Beträge ohne vorhergehende Mahnung eingezogen und erforderlichenfalls beigetrieben. Die Zwangsvollstreckungskosten fallen dem Zahlungspflichtigen zur Last.

Herrn
Frau Hilde Frühauf

in Meiningen

FIGURE 7 Notice from the Tax Office in Meiningen, dated December 7, 1938, concerning the required Surrender of Jewish Property as "Atonement Payment" to be made by Hilde Frühauf.

offered to them. Felix dissolved his wholesale leather-goods business. An acquaintance took over the warehouse at a bargain price and, to top it all off, paid for it in installments. With that the family's economic foundation was gone, and they had to live off their capital. Jews who were less well off were able to eke out an existence only with the help of Jewish welfare.

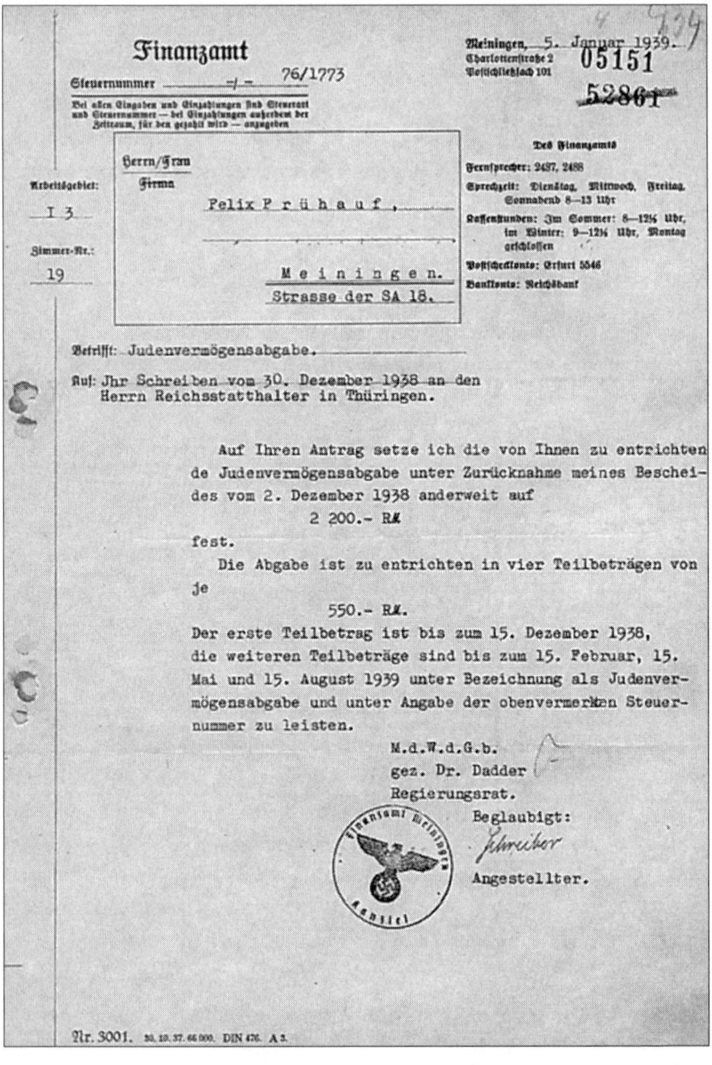

Finanzamt

Steuernummer ___ -/ - ___ 76/1773

Bei allen Eingaben und Einzahlungen sind Steuerart
und Steuernummer — bei Einzahlungen außerdem der
Zeitraum, für den gezahlt wird — anzugeben

Meiningen, 5. Januar 1939.
Charlottenstraße 2
Postschließfach 101   **05151**

5286

Arbeitsgebiet:
I 3

Zimmer-Nr.:
19

Herrn/Frau
Firma

Felix P r ü h a u f ,

M e i n i n g e n.
Strasse der SA 18.

Des Finanzamts

Fernsprecher: 2437, 2438

Sprechzeit: Dienstag, Mittwoch, Freitag,
Sonnabend 8—13 Uhr

Kassenstunden: Im Sommer: 8—12½ Uhr,
im Winter: 9—12½ Uhr, Montag
geschlossen

Postscheckkonto: Erfurt 5546

Bankkonto: Reichsbank

Betrifft: Judenvermögensabgabe.

Auf: Jhr Schreiben vom 30. Dezember 1938 an den
Herrn Reichsstatthalter in Thüringen.

   Auf Ihren Antrag setze ich die von Ihnen zu entrichten
de Judenvermögensabgabe unter Zurücknahme meines Beschei-
des vom 2. Dezember 1938 anderweit auf

   2 200.- RM

fest.
   Die Abgabe ist zu entrichten in vier Teilbeträgen von
je

   550.- RM.

Der erste Teilbetrag ist bis zum 15. Dezember 1938,
die weiteren Teilbeträge sind bis zum 15. Februar, 15.
Mai und 15. August 1939 unter Bezeichnung als Judenvermögensabgabe und unter Angabe der obenvermerkten Steuernummer zu leisten.

   M.d.W.d.G.b.
   gez. Dr. Dadder
   Regierungsrat.

   Beglaubigt:

   Schreiber

   Angestellter.

Nr. 3001.   50, 10, 37. 66 000. DIN 476. A 5.

FIGURE 8 Notice from the Meiningen Tax Office of an adjustment in the amount of Jewish property to be surrendered by Felix Frühauf, dated January 5, 1939.

❧

Plans to Emigrate

In the summer of 1938 the family decided to leave Germany and emigrate to the United States. Helga, who had come home for a few days of vacation, was to go on ahead because, by a stroke of luck, a relative in Rochester sent her an affidavit on the basis of which she was able to register on October 18, 1938, to immigrate to the United States; she was assigned the number 47,591.

In early 1939 the German authorities did not issue the customary identity card to Hilde because, they said, she was born in the United States. But at the American consulate in Leipzig it was explained to her that what counted was the nationality of her husband, since she had married before 1922. Therefore, she was told, she was a German citizen and had lost her American citizenship. If she wanted to reinstate that citizenship, she would have to go to the United States and pass an examination there. Hilde immediately applied for a visitor's visa.

This situation opened up a hopeful prospect. Once in the United States, as an American citizen, Hilde could work to expedite the emigration of her family from Germany with the help of form number 633 ("Petition for Special Consideration for the Immediate Relatives of a U.S. Citizen," that is, husband, children, and parents). This petition would have made it possible for the Frühaufs to leave Germany for the United States as "nonquota" immigrants. Others had to register under the normal quota and then wait until their number came up.

The Paper War

All those who wanted to immigrate to the United States had to have relatives or acquaintances in America who would furnish affidavits of support, as well as written proof of their financial means and income. A security deposit had to be made in a bank by the United States citizen as a guarantee that sufficient funds would be available to take care of the immigrants once they were in the United States Furthermore, ship passages were to be booked in America and proof had to be provided that the tickets had been paid for and accommodations on board ship had actually been reserved; if necessary a deposit for the transport of baggage also had to be arranged.

Only after all these conditions had been met would the State Department in Washington, D.C., give its OK to the American consulate general in Berlin. And only then would the emigrants be summoned to receive their visas and to undergo medical examinations at the consulate. Their passports would be retained and then stamped with the required visa.

Before emigrants were allowed to leave the country, the German authorities required them to obtain a document certifying that they owed no outstanding taxes, loans, or the like, and to show receipts indicating they had paid the compulsory property levies (*Vermögensabgaben*) and the so-called Reich Flight Tax (*Reichsfluchtsteuer*). Emigrants also had to provide proof that all their debts to the Jewish community had been met and to present a police certificate canceling their registration as residents.

Renewing Hilde's American Citizenship

Hilde Frühauf began to prepare for her big journey; in February 1939 she asked her daughter Helga to come back from Berlin so that she could make some of the clothes needed for the trip and also to help her grandmother keep house while Hilde was in America.

Hilde received her visa on May 20, 1939, after the residents' registration office had certified that Mrs. Johanna, called Hilde, "Sara" Frühauf, née Schwerin, born August 7, 1892, in New York, had been officially registered with the police in Meiningen from January 1, 1920, to March 6, 1939; and after the Jewish Community in Erfurt had certified that her "regular contribution fees" had been paid up to December 31, 1939, and that on March 30, 1939, she had also paid an additional special contribution (an emigration tax) of 192 Reichsmarks,

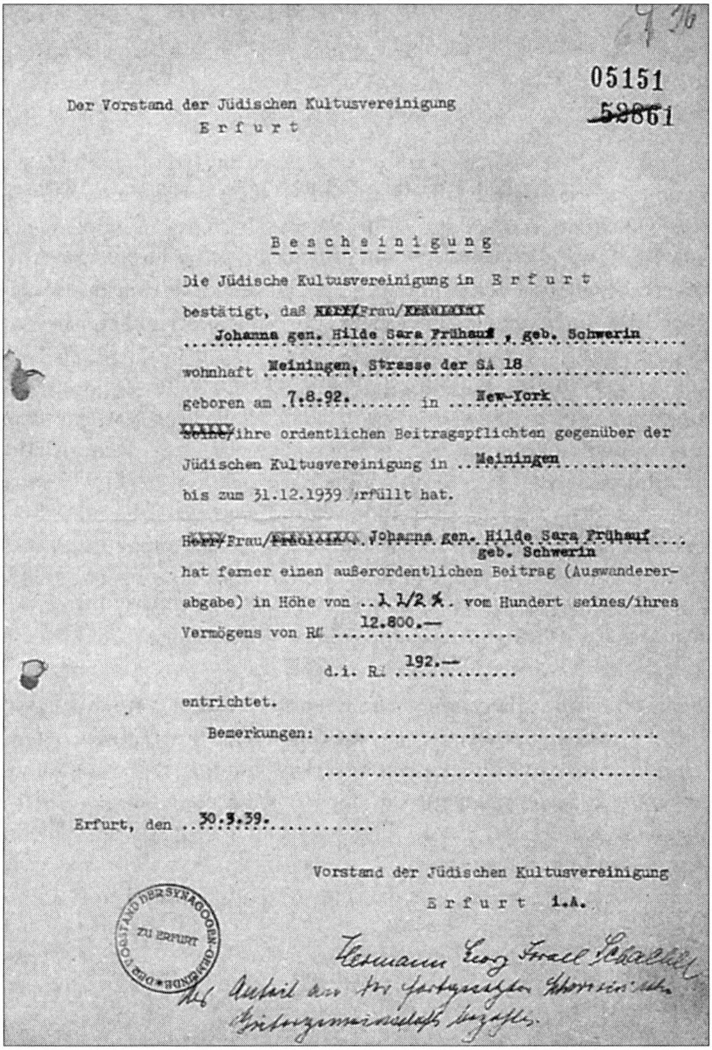
05151
~~59861~~

Der Vorstand der Jüdischen Kultusvereinigung
E r f u r t

B e s c h e i n i g u n g

Die Jüdische Kultusvereinigung in E r f u r t
bestätigt, daß ~~Herr~~/Frau/~~Fräulein~~
Johanna gen. Hilde Sara Frühauf, geb. Schwerin
wohnhaft Meiningen, Strasse der SA 18
geboren am 7.8.92. in New-York
~~seine~~/ihre ordentlichen Beitragspflichten gegenüber der
Jüdischen Kultusvereinigung in Meiningen
bis zum 31.12.1939 erfüllt hat.

~~Herr~~/Frau/~~Fräulein~~ Johanna gen. Hilde Sara Frühauf
geb. Schwerin
hat ferner einen außerordentlichen Beitrag (Auswandererabgabe) in Höhe von 1 1/2 % vom Hundert seines/ihres
Vermögens von RM 12.800.—
d.i. RM 192.—
entrichtet.

Bemerkungen: ....

Erfurt, den 30.3.39.

Vorstand der Jüdischen Kultusvereinigung
E r f u r t i.A.

DER VORSTAND DER SYNAGOGEN-GEMEINDE ZU ERFURT

FIGURE 9. A certificate from the Jewish Community in Erfurt verifying that Hilde Frühauf had paid the regular compulsory contribution as well as an extra contribution of 1-1/2 percent of her assets (levied on those who emigrated) to the Jewish Community of Meiningen; the document is dated March 30, 1939.

representing 1.5 percent of her assets, which amounted 12,800 marks.

The passage on the ship, including a return ticket, was booked in the firm belief that Hilde would be back in three months. On May

30, 1939, Hilde left Germany on what would be the last voyage of the *Columbus*, one of the three largest ships of the German Lloyd Company. Although she had paid for a first-class ticket and the ship was only half full, she was forced to occupy a third class cabin. All complaints to the captain were futile.

Hilde's arrival in New York—she was officially registered there as of June 1939—coincided with the start of a three-month-long court recess. This meant a crucial loss of time since she could not apply for renewal of her citizenship until the fall. She rented a furnished room at 559 West 164th Street and worked as a housekeeper for an immigrant couple from Berlin, the owner of the Scherk Company (a firm that made face lotions) and his wife.

Salvaging What They Could

Even before Hilde's departure, the Nazi state had seized the valuables of its Jewish population. On February 21, 1939, an order was issued that all gold, silver, platinum, and precious stones were to be handed over within fourteen days. The exceptions were one's wedding ring and/or that of a deceased spouse, gold teeth in use, one silver bracelet, one watch of up to 100 marks in value at the time of purchase, silver objects worth up to 200 marks (and weighing no more than 40 grams [1.4 oz.] each), and two four-piece sets of cutlery per person. Those who were emigrating were forbidden by law to take with them any jewelry or valuables, except for a knife, a spoon, a fork, wedding rings, and a watch.

During this time, in order to salvage what they could, the Frühaufs paid 1,000 marks to the wife of a lawyer friend in Berlin who used the money to have Hilde's jewelry copied in silver and imitation stones. The lawyer and his wife also agreed to try to get the genuine jewelry to America. During a visit to Romania, they planned to entrust the valuables to a jeweler there. But once in Romania, the transaction seemed too risky, and they took the pieces home again. In the fall of that year Felix transported the jewelry, concealed in some used soap bars and hidden in the false bottom of his suitcase (a pearl necklace was sewn into the hem of his trousers) to Berlin. His wife's cousin, the antique dealer Alfred Grossmann, smuggled these nine pieces of jewelry in a little evening bag to New York. When Hilde telegraphed the prearranged message to Meiningen, "Mrs. Rosenkranz has arrived with all her family, 9 people altogether," they knew that the pearl necklace, watch, bracelets, brooches, and rings had reached her safely.

The Frühauf silver flatware, candlesticks, silver bowls and platters, and the coffee and tea sets and trays—some had considerable sterling content—were appraised on September 2, 1939, by a certified master goldsmith, Eugen Mayer, in Arnstadt. The items were stored as "the dowry of the American Hilde Frühauf" in safety deposit box number 886 in the vault of the Verbandssparkasse, a savings bank in Meiningen, thereby temporarily keeping them out of the government's reach. The articles could have been redeemed within a year with foreign currency, but the sum required was so formidable that Felix's uncle, Meyer Vomberg, who lived in Michigan and whom they had asked to send the money, refused. And so, at the end of August 1940, the valuables went to the municipal pawnshop of Berlin, where they were auctioned off on August 18, 1941, in "fulfillment of the required obligation for Jews to turn in their property" (see documents 1 and 2).*

*Documents are grouped together at the back of the book, following the final chapter.

❖

September 1, 1939:

Hitler Starts a World Conflagration

In the fall of 1939 the Nazi state put a freeze on all Jewish assets with its law to block Jewish property (*Sicherungs-Anordnung*). Felix was ordered to open a "blocked account with restricted availability" within five days in a foreign exchange bank by the foreign exchange department of the Regional Office of the Finance Ministry of Thüringen in Rudolstadt. Although they were allowed to keep other existing postal or savings accounts, Jews had to deposit any money they received in the limited availability blocked account. Unless they were given special approval, they were only permitted to withdraw a fixed allowance. For the Frühaufs, the allowance was 200 marks a month. This subsistence allotment was raised to 410 marks on September 29.

It was forbidden to have any cash over and above that. Money to pay taxes, penalties, fees for notaries, medical costs, contributions to the Jewish Community and to religious and social institutions, as well as the costs for lawyers, travel, and other expenses connected with the emigration process, could be withdrawn only from the blocked account (see document 3).

On September 20, 1939, Jews were forbidden to own radio receivers and had to turn in all radios in their possession. In order to keep Jews from acquiring new sets, dealers had to register every person who purchased a radio. Telephones in Jewish homes also were confiscated. On September 1 a curfew was imposed, and Jews were not permitted to leave their homes after 8 P.M., or 9 P.M. in the summer months. In October the following decree was issued: "All Jews who do not immediately comply with any order whatsoever or demonstrate behavior that is detrimental to the state will be arrested immediately and placed in a concentration camp."

Ration cards for the purchase of clothing, which had at first been allocated to Jews, were revoked. Now, whenever they needed an item of apparel, they had to apply for a ration coupon and present the worn-out article of clothing.

On December 1 special food rations were reduced. Consequently, during the time between December 18, 1939, and January 14, 1940, Jews received less meat and butter and no cocoa or rice; from January 15 to February 4, 1940, they received no meat and no vegetables.

Jews were not allowed to set foot in German stores. They were assigned to shop at designated stores. For the Jews of Meiningen some of these stores were scattered in neighboring villages: for instance, the butcher was in Helba and the greengrocer in Weidig. Since shopping time was limited to the hour between 7 and 8 A.M. during the summer as well as the winter months, it was often impossible—even if a bicycle was used—to take care of more than one shopping errand a day. The dairyman gave them a particularly rough time: Often, even though the Jews had been waiting in line since 7 A.M.— standing behind the "members of the master race," as required—he would announce scornfully, as the clock struck eight, "I can't help you any more today."

Support and Help from Fellow Citizens

Still there were some non-Jewish Germans who showed humanity and courage, especially during this difficult time. The Frühaufs' cleaning woman remained loyal to the family; she exchanged her beef for the pork that the butcher—on orders, he said—had wrapped up for them, and she warned the butcher that her own large family would no longer buy their meat from him if it happened again. Once when Grandmother Lina was standing in despair in front of her empty pots, the bell rang, and a farmer from Walldorf put a baby lamb, some lamb fat, and butter on the Frühaufs' table.

Their neighbors the Reichenbachers, a shoemaker and his family whose workshop was located on land owned by the Frühaufs, continued to stand by them. Repeatedly they sent over food. Helga's brother, Rudolf, reciprocated by secretly helping the shoemaker evenings and nights when there was more work than he could handle. The Reichenbachers also took a further risk by letting the Frühaufs use their telephone. If there was a phone call for Felix, they would let him know through a prearranged series of knocks on the Frühaufs' door.

At the shoemaker's home, Helga met Käthe Hauschild, the wife of a German army officer who, on the spur of the moment, invited the young Jewish woman to visit her. Helga, flustered at first, thought it impossible to have a social relationship with an army officer's wife, and at the start her father also argued against it, but Käthe did not give up, and soon the two young women became friends. Käthe's companionship provided almost the only bright spot in Helga's sad existence. Whenever possible, she would stealthily walk the ten minutes to Käthe's house after dark, and from time to time she even stayed overnight or an entire day. If visitors came unexpectedly, Helga would lock herself into the bathroom, and if someone wanted to use the toilet, Käthe would pretend that her two-year-old son, Lutz, had lost the key. Whenever another wave of arrests was impending, Käthe also hid Helga's father in her apartment for several days. Her husband, who was stationed in France, knew about this. Käthe shared with Helga all the rare delicacies he sent or brought back when he came home on leave.

An Immigrant in New York

With the news of Hitler's invasion of Poland on September 1, 1939, Hilde's worries about her family in Germany became almost unbearable. As soon as the court recess ended that month, she started her struggle with U.S. authorities for the reinstatement of her citizenship and the immigration of her family. Above all, she had to obtain the necessary affidavits of support. She went knocking on the doors of all her relatives and acquaintances, valiantly begging for their help. But most of them were recent immigrants themselves and had not yet gained an economic foothold in America—for example, her sister-in-law, Martha Joachimsthal, and her brother, Monroe Schwerin, who was scraping along as a salesman and needed every penny of the money he earned for his wife and children.

Many Jews who had been in America for a long time did not yet realize the extent of the persecution in Hitler's Germany and refused to believe the reports of horrors that were trickling through. At last Hilde found a well-to-do sponsor in the person of Meyer Vomberg, her mother-in-law's brother, who was more than eighty years old. He was the owner of the Vomberg Company (clothing, hats, and furnishings) in Charlotte, Michigan, and he was prepared to help.

Meanwhile the year had drawn to an end. The protracted waiting for her certification as a U.S. citizen brought Hilde to the edge of despair. Tragically, in February 1940 the first signs of a serious illness surfaced—cancer, treated successfully at first with radiation.

Then Hilde's New York lawyer, a Mr. Wirth, told her that she had already passed her examination for American citizenship in court on October 11, 1939 (shortly after the court recess ended). The document was to be delivered to her on January 6, 1940, and on January 29 Hilde Frühauf took her oath of allegiance. Finally it was done! Washington executed the document on March 20. She immediately

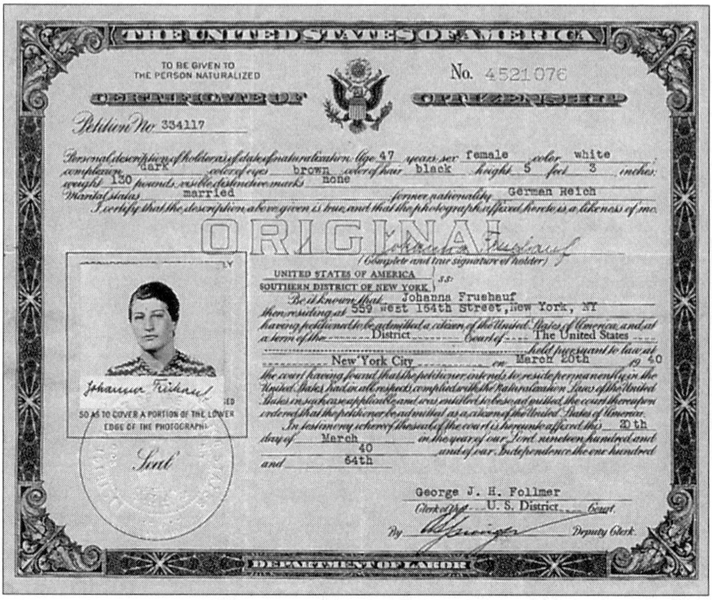
THE UNITED STATES OF AMERICA

TO BE GIVEN TO THE PERSON NATURALIZED

No. 4521076

CERTIFICATE OF CITIZENSHIP

Petition No. 334117

Personal description of holder as of date of naturalization: Age 47 years; sex female color white complexion dark color of eyes brown color of hair black height 5 feet 3 inches; weight 130 pounds; visible distinctive marks none

Marital status married former nationality German Reich

I certify that the description above given is true, and that the photograph affixed hereto is a likeness of me.

ORIGINAL

(Complete and true signature of holder)

UNITED STATES OF AMERICA } SS:
SOUTHERN DISTRICT OF NEW YORK }

Be it known that Johanna Fruehauf then residing at 559 West 164th Street, New York, NY having petitioned to be admitted a citizen of the United States of America, and at a term of the District Court of The United States held pursuant to law at New York City on March 20th 1940 the court having found that the petitioner intends to reside permanently in the United States, had in all respects complied with the Naturalization Laws of the United States in such case applicable and was entitled to be so admitted, the court thereupon ordered that the petitioner be admitted as a citizen of the United States of America.

In testimony whereof the seal of the court is hereunto affixed this 20th day of March in the year of our Lord nineteen hundred and 40 and of our Independence the one hundred and 64th

SO AS TO COVER A PORTION OF THE LOWER EDGE OF THE PHOTOGRAPH

Seal

George J. H. Follmer
Clerk of the U. S. District Court.
By Deputy Clerk.

DEPARTMENT OF LABOR

FIGURE 10. Hilde Frühauf's U.S. Naturalization Certificate dated March 20, 1940, bearing her citizenship number 4521076.

telegraphed Germany, giving her family the number on her Certificate of Citizenship—4521076—that was so vital to their survival.

In a letter Hilde complained bitterly about the "snail's pace" at which Washington worked—the entire procedure had taken from fall to spring—and also that one could not simply make a copy of the document, which she could then send on to them; it had to be a certified and notarized copy. But now at last, form 633 could be filed, asking that her family be permitted to immigrate on a nonquota basis.

The telegram she sent from America alarmed the police in Weimar. Two officials came to Meiningen and asked for an explanation of this mysterious number, 4521076. They considered Felix's answer that it was his American wife's naturalization number questionable. Only the intervention of Felix's friend, police officer Thrän, appeased them. "I told you from the start that everything's in order with Felix. You may as well leave now," Thrän said to them. And so Helga and Ruldolf's fear that their father would be taken away again was laid to rest.

There was a feeling of euphoria in the Frühauf household. Now things were moving again! They could start to pack their bags. On April 18, 1940, Felix ordered a "lift" (a large container made of wood) for their move. A list was drawn up containing 100 items belonging to "the American Hilde Frühauf" and six items belonging to her husband. The authorities crossed off 42 of these because, according to regulations, "no items acquired after 1932 could be taken abroad." They must either be "sold privately" or handed over to the Erfurt branch office of the Reich Organization of Jews in Germany (*Reichsvereinigung der Juden in Deutschland*). The Frühaufs were able to sell off some of their things; the rest were given away (see documents 4–10).

The Desperate Struggle with the Bureaucracy

Hilde's letters from New York reveal the trials and tribulations she endured during those days. They disclose the nerve-racking strain of being at the mercy of the bureaucratic machinery and how American immigration authorities at all levels placed obstacles in her path. Probably also driven by her deteriorating health, Hilde frantically attempted to obtain the visas, which "they are investigating especially thoroughly now," she wrote on May 20. Even though the U.S. Consulate in Berlin had already informed Washington by telegraph that all the documents were in order, the Hilfsverein* now cabled that "everything is to be done from this end [that is, in America]." Hilde cabled the U.S. Consul in Leipzig, asking him "to take the family of an American citizen under his protection." It was all in vain.

A whole year had passed since her arrival in New York. And now the application procedure had to be started from the beginning and the required documents had to be submitted all over again!

Hilde waited anxiously for letters from her family and wrote long epistles home to her "beloved four," as she called her husband, the two children, and her mother. She spent what time she had—between treatments by physicians and days in the hospital and as

---

*Hilfsverein der Juden in Deutschland (Relief Organization of Jews in Germany).

much as her waning strength would allow—running to various offices, to the Hilfsverein, to the Council of Jewish Women, and to the American Jewish Joint Distribution Committee. She asked for advice and help from her acquaintances and friends, from anyone she could find. At least overseas mail was moving faster now that America had air mail "Clipper Service."

New York, May 20, 1940

My beloved four,
. . . . I won't be sending letters by sea mail anymore; air mail leaves weekly. . . . I feel better every day; as I wrote you before, I am not getting treatments any more, and only have to go to the hospital every 14 days for observation, and the doctors are very pleased with me. . . . There is absolutely no reason to worry any more. . . . My worries are of another sort—what's the quickest way to get you to join me here. From the cable you saw that I certainly am not asleep on the job and that I am thinking night and day about what can be done. Unfortunately, the documents were examined too thoroughly in Washington and they were found insufficient for four people. As soon as I get them back from Washington, they have to be reprocessed. I hope that we can start on that in the next few days. I've already written to your uncle but have not yet received a definitive reply. Everything takes time here. "Take it easy" is the Americans' favorite expression. And I am in "despair" not just occasionally, but all the time. . . . I'm going to move heaven and earth again. . . . A lot of the blame also has to go to our relatives, for letting me wait so long for the affidavits, more than 4 weeks, and then they didn't fill them out properly. . . .

But not even a declaration of Meyer Vomberg's wealth was enough for the authorities in Washington. The documents were returned and had to be resubmitted, furnished with better affidavits of support.

Running around to the authorities, all those telegrams, and the costs for doctors and the hospital swallowed Hilde's funds. As she wrote in one of her letters, eighty cents for a one-way trip to Long Island is a lot of money when one is earning about thirty cents an hour. To keep her head above water, she took on piecework at home; and three or four times a month she worked for an acquaintance, for which she received ten dollars a month. The fifty dollars she was paid by Mrs. Rosenkranz for her help was a real godsend. Hilde even intended to put something aside so that her family wouldn't starve during the first days after their arrival.

On July 9, 1940, Hilde wrote:

My beloved four,
It's convenient that there are now 3 Clippers a week leaving from here. . . . I don't feel very well again. It is still the reaction to the radiation treatments and my nerves can't take it . . . . In addition there is also a swelling on my neck . . . it has to be treated and kept under observation. For that reason I have to spend a few days in the hospital again . . . , which ought to be something of a vacation for me. . . . Mrs. St. Goar has taken the matter in hand together with the lawyer and the [American Jewish Joint Distribution] Committee, and we all hope that now we will soon reach our goal. The telegram from the consulate is being processed by the Committee, and we are also working on booking your passages. I hope that your Uncle [Meyer Vomberg] won't make us wait so long this time. You can depend on this: everything will be processed in the best and quickest way we know, except that at the moment I can't run around to do it myself. . . . I only wish you could take a different route than this big tour. I don't want to do anything too hastily; once I have the money available, everything can be booked and cabled quickly. . . .

The next day, July 10, Hilde continued her letter from Port Washington:

. . . . And in the meantime a lot of things have changed for me. I wasn't sent to the hospital, but rather to a small, charming sanatorium on Long Island, three quarters of an hour from New York, out in the country and right near the ocean. . . .

It turned out that Hilde's cancer was incurable. In spite of that, she found new hope for her family.

> . . . The lady from the Committee who is working on the last cable from Leipzig thinks that you will be asked to appear [to pick up your visas] after that, and she will set everything in motion to get you ship's tickets . . . .

By "big tour" Hilde meant the possibility her husband was considering of traveling to the United States via Russia and Japan. This odyssey by Trans-Siberian Railway—in sealed cars so that no one would get off en route—would take them to Vladivostok and from there by ship to Yokohama. Jews were also trying to find their way to America by way of Shanghai and Cuba. Since no visa was required for China, this route was open to all. But it was so prohibitively expensive, few could afford it.

The Hilfsverein and emigration advisors—mostly Jewish lawyers—who helped their clients through the legal jungle, counseled them to pursue simultaneously a number of different ways of leaving the country, in case one or the other were to fall through. For that reason Felix had several irons in the fire.

On July 16 Hilde wrote from Port Washington:

> . . . I can't rest easy until everything has been arranged for you. From the outset ours has been a very complicated affair. . . . I hope that you, my dear, have received the confirmation [of the naturalization certificate], that is, the one that the Council [of Jewish Women] sent through the diplomatic pouch. Another one is being processed by Dr. Moses and the Council. Moses [the lawyer Hilde hired] is going to Washington again, and then I hope everything will work out. Also with regard to Form 633 . . . . Everything, but everything, has been arranged, and we are also waiting to hear any day now with regard to the ship passages: it's in the best of hands. Just don't lose your head now. . . . And so, even though you have been asking me for the confirmation ever since October, it could only be done as of March; in Washington they work very slowly. . . .

On July 20, 1940, Arthur Vomberg, Uncle Meyer Vomberg's son, personally deposited the money for the Frühaufs' ship tickets at American Express in New York. He was informed that the amount of 350 dollars already paid the year before was not lost, but that at the moment it was not available!

On July 21 Hilde wrote:

> . . . I haven't been this happy in a long time. . . . Arthur Vomberg from Charlotte is here. . . . I greeted my new cousin, and I must say I am more and more impressed with the family. A splendid, charming man, 46 years old, quite American, but very nice. . . . He came here especially because of our problem. He went to the Council of Jewish Women; he intended to speak with the lawyer; and he was also at American Express and ordered and paid for the 4 ship tickets for you. American Express in Berlin will get in touch with you, dear Felix. . . . And this week I also want to extract the confirmation from Washington, finally. You will need it for the passport, the baggage authorization, etc. . . . I am fine; everyone is amazed how much better I look already. . . . "

On July 25 Hilde informed them that her letter and a statement by a notary public that he had "personally seen her naturalization certificate" had been sent to Leipzig. She asked her New York lawyer, Dr. Moses, to send another duplicate of form 633 and Uncle Meyer Vomberg's deposit to Berlin.

> My beloved four,
> . . . In the meantime the letter that Mr. St. Goar wrote to Leipzig for me will have arrived. In that letter a notary public attests that he has personally seen my naturalization certificate. . . . Why haven't you been requested to appear [at the U.S. Consulate] yet? Things have got to move ahead sooner or later. . . . Mrs. St. Goar had no other news for me except to tell me that my Form 633 was going through the regular channels in Washington, that one had to be patient. The Council is also working on it, and they're pushing Moses along. The Council

is so enthusiastic about our [Michigan] relatives, who immediately declared themselves ready to pay for the ship tickets. . . .
Since I may be staying here [at the sanatorium] for a while, I
am probably going to give up my room, because paying for
both places costs too much. Perhaps I shall stay here until I
rent an apartment for us, maybe near Walter—we'll work it
out somehow. First we have to get to that point. I was sure I'd
be receiving a cable this week, now that the ship ticket money
has been made available. In case you haven't had any word yet,
get in touch with American Express right away because they
must surely have received the notification by now. Then take
the notification to the U.S. Consulate; that is what they want:
to see paid-for tickets.—Have your things been inspected and
packed in the meantime? Don't delay any more now and take
the first ship that comes along. The trip via Russia must be
very strenuous. . . .

Did you also put my silk shawl on the list? It was always at
the back of the linen closet—I mean the one with the long
fringes. They are very much back in style here . . . Go through
your things again very thoroughly and don't bring anything
unnecessary; it's only an extra burden. . . . I hope you haven't
forgotten the medicine cabinets that are hanging in Grandma
and Uncle's house. . . . I hope next week we'll know more
about what's ahead for us. Keep your spirits up! Stay well!

Everything Depends on a Single Piece of Paper!

On August 9 Hilde's lawyer told her that he finally had received the
notification from Washington and that everything now depended on
one document from her brother, Monroe. After she received a
telegram from Leipzig, she was convinced that things would work
out all right. She wrote from New York on August 10, 1940:

. . . In the meantime quite a lot has happened. Martha probably wrote to you—I asked her to do that so that you wouldn't
worry. The reaction to the radiation I have received has been
especially hard on me, and this time it was so bad that I had to

stay in the clinic several days . . . . Now I have been placed in a [convalescent] home in New York, and I see and hear more than I did when I was alone. At the moment I have difficulties with eating. But I think I will make up for everything once I am surrounded by your love and care. I hope that everything will work out more quickly now, for yesterday the lawyer told me all that's needed now is one document from Monroe . . . and I hope that Monroe will move heaven and earth to prepare his document as soon as possible. I wrote him about it last evening. Since our affidavits are not all that impressive, they want affidavits of support from the closest relatives. There is no sense in cabling the money from my bank account since it is ridiculously little. Besides, the 3,000 dollars from Uncle [Meyer Vomberg] were supposed to have been transferred, as well as the guarantee of the ship tickets. . . . After Monroe sends the new affidavit next week, I think that it will be cabled over immediately . . . Besides Mr. Wirth, the lawyer, wrote to Moses and he will probably also send a confirmation from Washington; he ordered it done immediately. . . .

Yesterday I also received the telegram from Leipzig; they are really considerate. But I think that form 633 will surely work out all right now. . . . You see, it doesn't work any faster for other people either. The people for whom it's expedited are those who have big incomes and are sending for only one person, someone like their mother, to join them. We have waited so long now, you may as well come over together. . . . I think that by now the confirmation must have finally arrived in the diplomatic mail. Then all of you will come here together. . . .

Not Quite Yet . . .

On August 15, 1940, the lawyer Moses again asked for Hilde's citizenship certificate so that he could obtain the final statement in Washington. Hilde hoped that her brother's affidavit would arrive by August 22. Four days later the American Consulate in Leipzig informed Felix that it had received a letter dated July 8, 1940, from the National Refugee Service, Inc., 169 West 46th Street, New York, according to which Mrs. Hilde Frühauf's sworn declaration certifying

> that she had been granted American citizenship on March 20,
> 1940 in the district court of the southern district of New York,
> New York has arrived in Washington, and that her application
> for Immigration Visas (Form No. 633) is currently on file in
> Washington.—In order for the Consulate [in Leipzig] to
> receive confirmation from the State Department in Washing-
> ton of the actual naturalization of Mrs. Frühauf as an Ameri-
> can citizen, the Consulate is prepared to send a telegram to the
> State Department. . . . —If you agree with this arrangement,
> would you please transmit the amount of 42.20 Reichsmarks
> to the Consulate to cover the cost of sending the telegram and
> a reply from the State Department. . . .

Hilde wrote from New York on August 15, 1940:

My beloved four,
I am writing with a pencil because I feel that it's easier for me.
This time it really took a lot out of me, and my recuperation is
very slow. But the main thing is that I feel some improvement.
. . . Dr. Moses sent me a message yesterday saying that he had
received a cable and that he wanted my citizenship certificate
again. Surely the right confirmation will finally be sent out
now. Monroe wrote that he is working hard on the affidavit. I
hope that he will finally send it off next week. Filling out documents can't always be done in a jiffy. So don't worry, I'll make
every effort to have everything done as quickly as possible. For
once it's got to work out all right. . . .
     Some glands in my throat have now become conspicuously
swollen, and that swelling will go back down again very slowly.
I have visitors all the time. Please send my mail to Blumenfelds
[who had taken Hilde in to stay with them], since I don't
know how long [I] will be staying here. . . . I can't understand
why you haven't heard anything from American Express.
Uncle sent 10 dollars specifically for [them] to cable [you].
On July 20th Arthur arranged everything. So it would be
worthwhile for you to go to Berlin. . . . The Committee says

that everything has been done properly and all is in order now.
I am sorry that I've been doing everything, but everything,
wrong and that the confirmation has never worked out.
Apparently I've hit a streak of bad luck. Walter pulled out as
well. All relatives are alike. At first they are happy [to help] and
the next time their happiness is diluted. . . . German lawyers
here have no idea at all [about what to do], and it's the same if
one asks business people; that is also why Monroe doesn't
know the ins and outs. . . .

I am very proud that [I] can write these 1 1/2 pages without
stopping, something I couldn't have done last week. Herta has
just now come back from seeing Moses; he is working on the
confirmation. That is why I had to give him my [citizenship]
certificate again so that he could get the Statement in Washington. . . . I hope to God that soon now everything will be
ready. I also hope to get some good news from you soon. I
hope you are well. My beloved four, I embrace you tenderly
with all my heart and send you kisses,
Your mother and Hilde.

It was her last letter. Ten days later she died. To the end she had
bravely kept the seriousness of her illness from her family. She asked
all those around her not to tell anyone in Germany that she had
incurable cancer. She had fought with superhuman strength and
spared no effort to bring her family to America. And she almost succeeded: The day after her death the documents for the form 633
process were completed. The affidavit from Hilde's brother, Monroe
Schwerin, was issued by his bank in Sheboygan on August 26, 1940,
and notarized—all of it too late.

Emigration at Risk

On August 29, 1940, Recha Frühauf, Felix's sister in Berlin, received
the following telegram: HILDE PASSED AWAY—BURIED WEDNESDAY—
NOTIFY FELIX GENTLY—WONT AFFECT IMMIGRATION—MARTHA

"Won't affect . . ."—how wrong can you be! It seemed, in fact,
the immigration authorities in Washington had nothing more
urgent to do than to immediately inform the U.S. Consulate in

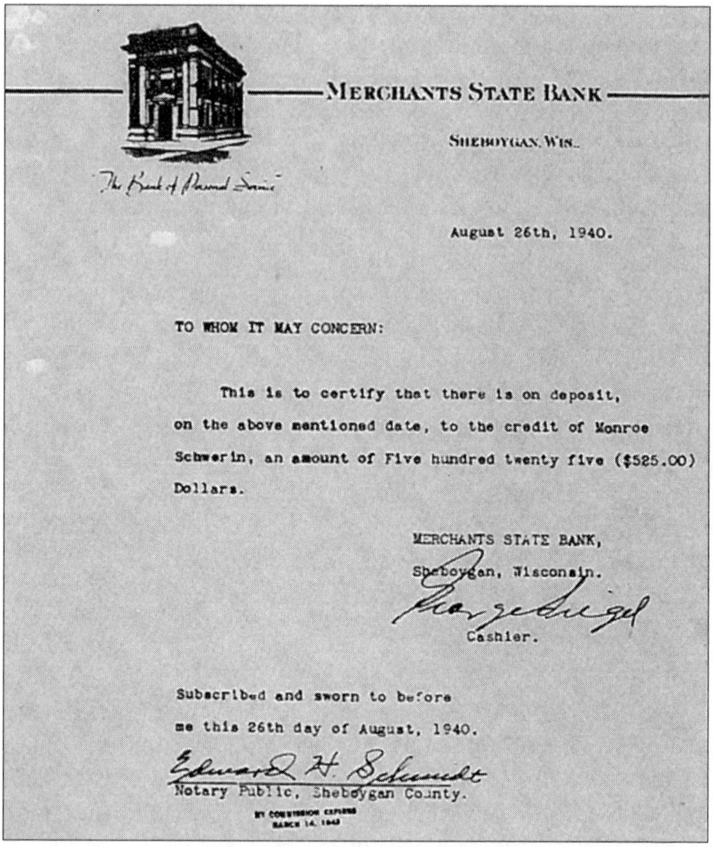

MERCHANTS STATE BANK

SHEBOYGAN, WIS.

August 26th, 1940.

TO WHOM IT MAY CONCERN:

This is to certify that there is on deposit, on the above mentioned date, to the credit of Monroe Schwerin, an amount of Five hundred twenty five ($525.00) Dollars.

MERCHANTS STATE BANK,
Sheboygan, Wisconsin.

Cashier.

Subscribed and sworn to before me this 26th day of August, 1940.

Notary Public, Sheboygan County.

FIGURE 11. A notarized letter from the Merchants State Bank in Sheboygan, Wisconsin, certifying that the amount of $525 was on deposit as of August 26, 1940, to the credit of Monroe Schwerin, Hilde Frühauf's brother, who lived in the United States.

Berlin, by telephone, of Hilde's death with the express instruction that her family could now no longer be given priority as immigrants. This bad news was disclosed to the Frühaufs by Consul van Roosen. He already had the notice for them to pick up their visas lying on his desk but was not allowed to send it off now. With tears in his eyes he explained to the dismayed Frühaufs, "If Washington had sent the information by telegram or letter instead of by phone, I would have given you the visas, and you could have left."

All efforts had been in vain—all their hopes were dashed.

✧

Getting Out of Germany on the
Regular Quota

As mentioned earlier, a relative in Rochester had made out an affidavit of support for Helga in 1938. Consequently, she had been registered for emigration since October 18 of that year under number 47,591, and it would probably have been her turn to be called up by now. Felix and Rudolf were registered on January 26, 1939, and assigned the numbers 60,119 and 65,261, respectively, and Grandmother Lina received her registration number on March 4, 1939. They were hoping now that they would all be selected to leave together.

Various relatives and acquaintances got involved, and there was a renewed flurry of letters and telegrams back and forth between Meiningen and America, reflecting the Frühaufs' desperate efforts to obtain the documents and the money required for their departure from Germany. At the same time this exchange also documents the family's hopeless entanglement in a maze of red tape.

On September 20, 1940, Hilde's brother, Monroe, wrote to ask about their quota numbers and when these had been assigned:

. . . We now hear from Martha that Hilde must have been well aware of how sick she was, even though the terminal nature of her illness became evident only in the final weeks. . . . Like Hilde, we always hoped that you would see each other again. . . . With regard to the affidavits and also the money for the ship passage, I have done everything I could possibly do. I have been informed by New York that passage for four people has been guaranteed. But we'll write to New York again about the entire matter. What [quota] number were you given by the consulate? You never wrote us about that. Isn't your number

due to come up soon? . . . This week we received the first
detailed letter from Erna in Rochester where she was sent by
the [American Jewish Joint Distribution] Committee, the
same way we were sent to Sheboygan. She writes that the local
Committee already arranged a job for her there. She doesn't
earn much, but it's enough to get by on. We were very happy
about this good news, especially in view of the fact that at
some point you probably will want to go there too, and we
know how the Committee there works. . . .

On October 5, 1940, Martha sent letters by airmail from her brother
Felix to the uncle in Michigan. The letters contained instructions
and telegrams from the Hilfsverein. Then she wrote to Felix:

. . . We immediately sent your letters and the telegrams from
the Hilfsverein to Uncle Meyer, and he must and will take care
of it. . . . We also wrote to Washington, although there's probably nothing to be gained by that anymore. Herta asked Washington urgently to send a cable to the Berlin Consulate and to
ask whether the documents they have are sufficient. And
Uncle Meyer is supposed to have the bank send a cable; we
sent him the money for a prepaid reply. And he is supposed to
send you, Felix, a duplicate of it. Nobody could find out where
the reply cables were. . . .

On October 17, 1940, Meyer Vomberg wrote that the affidavits
were still with Mr. Moses, the lawyer in New York. Moses had requested Hilde to ask her husband to contact his lawyer and to inquire about
the status of his case at the Emigration Office in Germany.
    It was touching to see how the more than eighty-year-old uncle
not only tried to take care of everything promptly, but how he labo-
riously mobilized the remnants of his German, writing to his
nephew in the old German Gothic script (see figs. 12a and 12b):

Dear Felix,
. . . Believe me, my family sympathizes deeply with you on the
death of dear Hilde, whom we all loved. . . . Now I am again
in correspondence with Herta in New York [and] will do every-

thing possible to help you. Last December Hilde wrote me that it would be better if I would send her $350 to help you with your emigration. I sent it in her name, and the American Express Co. sent it for you to their office in Amsterdam . . . Many regards to you and the children from us all. Uncle Meyer.

On October 20, 1940, Monroe Schwerin informed his brother-in-law, Felix, that he had provided an affidavit of support for his mother, Lina, and had then extended it to include Felix and his son and daughter. For weeks he had been trying to find out the status of these affidavits. They had to be revised, now that nonquota emigration was no longer possible. And to his mother he wrote:

> We can understand why you no longer feel like emigrating, but please consider that you could be a great help to Felix and the children, particularly at this time. There is no question whatsoever that you can come to stay with us at any time, even though we live very modestly. In any case, we would like you to come to America. We have been satisfied all along with our life here and we earn an honest living. . . . Marianne and I attend night school so we can learn English more quickly. . . . I would probably be able to speak [English] a good deal better if everyone in Sheboygan didn't speak German. Besides, our circle of friends consists of three German and three American families, and naturally we get together more often with the German-speaking ones. . . . Many thanks for the reply coupon.

Feverish Preparations for Emigration

In the meantime the Frühauf family had gathered Hilde's things together for the move—Hilde, "the American citizen." Because the news of her death had been transmitted only to Berlin, Felix took a chance and withheld this information from the local authorities in order to save their belongings and so as not to endanger the shipment of their goods overseas.

On September 19, 1940, everything was ready: All the furniture and other household articles as well as the emigrants' suitcases and

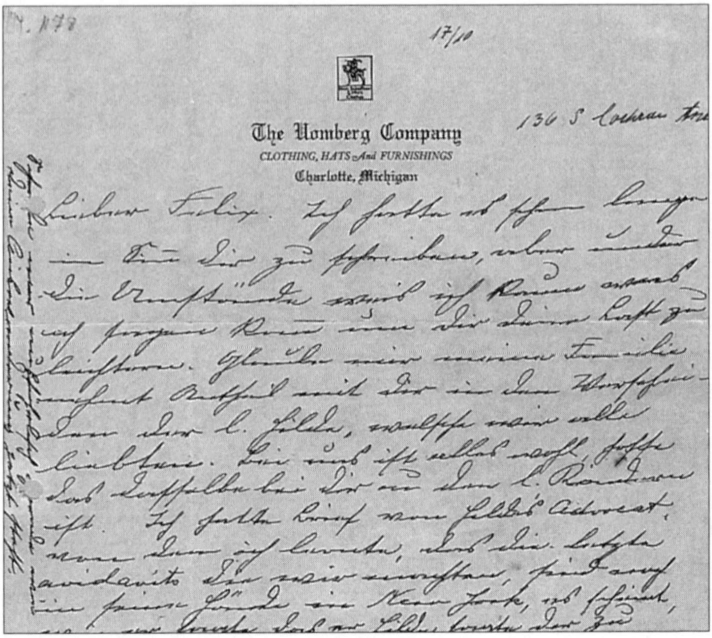
17/10

The Vomberg Company
CLOTHING, HATS And FURNISHINGS
Charlotte, Michigan

FIGURE 12A A letter written in German by Uncle Meyer Vomberg from Charlotte, Michigan, on October 17, 1940, to his nephew Felix Frühauf (front of letter).

hand luggage were examined and appraised (see documents 11–14). After that they were "requested" to make a nonrefundable payment of 400 marks to the German Gold and Discount Bank (Golddiskontbank) in Berlin (see documents 15–17). On October 23, 1940, the Frühaufs received permission "to transfer their goods which were to be sealed by the customs office." The railway shipping agent Werner Münch estimated the cost for supplying a three-meter lift at 490 marks and for a four-meter lift at 605 marks, plus the wages of the packers.

Another Tragic Blow

On the afternoon of October 30, 1940, Helga had gone on a brief errand to the post office. On her return, as she stepped into her grandmother's room, she froze in horror. The old woman had used

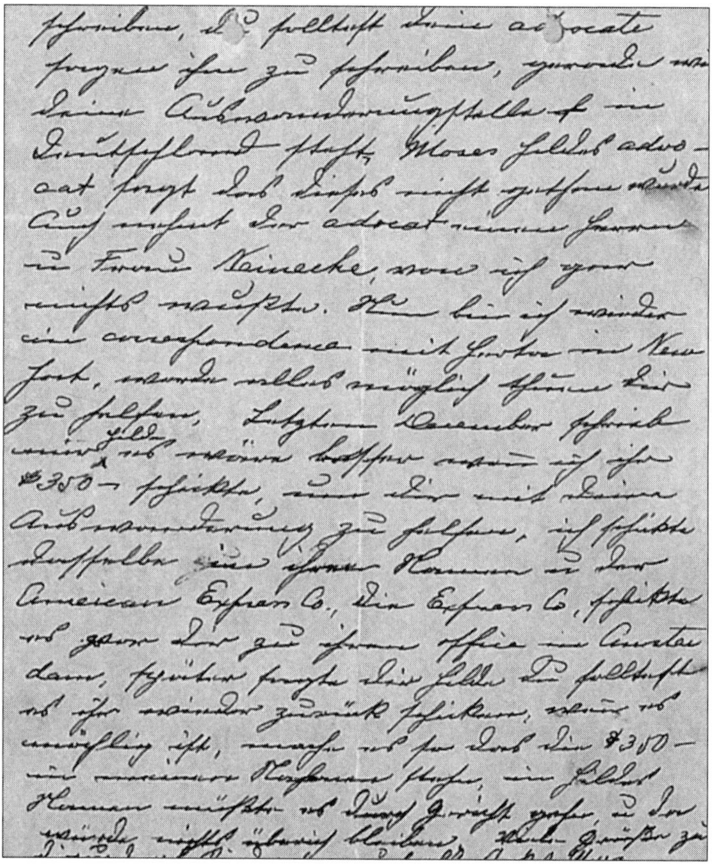

FIGURE 12B (back of letter).

her granddaughter's absence to commit suicide. She had hanged her-self on the crossbar of the window. Helga was never able to forget that image.

In her letter of farewell, seventy-year-old Lina Schwerin wrote that the Nazi terror and the misery of life as a Jew (in Germany) drove her to this desperate act. And most important of all, she added, after the death of her only daughter she could no longer muster the will or the strength to emigrate to America. She request-ed that she be cremated. Her ashes were interred in her husband's grave in Lüdenscheid.

There was little time for mourning. From now on Helga had to attend to all the household matters herself and, together with her father, prepare for the move.

A Race against Time

On November 1, 1940, a telegram from New York announced: CONFIRMATION OF DEPOSIT EN ROUTE—THROUGH MOSES. The lawyer sent the affidavits and the confirmation of the $3,000 deposit Meyer Vomberg had made in his bank via airmail on November 14. Once again the goal seemed within reach, provided the Frühaufs arrived in New York by January 1, 1941; otherwise the deposit would expire and would be returned to the uncle. In a letter to Felix, Vomberg asked, "[H]ow do you intend to travel out of Germany? I will do everything to help you. . . . I have also provided in my will. . . ." On November 14, 1940, Moses replied via airmail to Felix's letter of October 15:

For your immigration application I am sending you

1. the affidavit of your brother-in-law Monroe Schwerin. It was issued on August 26 . . .
2. the affidavit of your Uncle Meyer Vomberg.
3. the affidavit of his son, Arthur J. Vomberg, your cousin.
4. the Statement from the Eaton County Savings Bank that a deposit in the amount of $3,000 has been set up, payable in monthly installments that are to extend over two years.

The condition is that you arrive by January 1, 1941. Since this will not be possible, I shall ask your uncle to extend the deadline. All these papers were sent to Washington as documentary support for your late wife's application for preferential visas. That also explains the older dates. Unfortunately, the Department of Justice did not consider these affidavits to be sufficient, and as a result of her death the matter could not be finalized in Washington.

In the meantime, after inquiring at the U.S. Consulate in Berlin, we heard from the State Department in Washington, that you and your son Rudolf were registered on January 16, 1939; your daughter Helga as long ago as October 18, 1938, and Mrs. Lina Schwerin, your mother-in-law, not until March 4, 1939. Your daughter Helga's turn for an ordinary quota visa would be coming up now. . . . From now on, your applications must be made on the ordinary quota. That would also have been the case if your late wife's application had been approved. . . . I would also like to point out that [even] if you do not notify the Consulate of the death of your wife, this, now as before, would depend on the approval of Form No. 633, which is now, after the death of your wife, impossible to obtain. I should also like to point out that if you had arrived here on a non-quota or preferential visa after the death of your wife, you might have jeopardized your status . . . .

I advise you to write the following letter to the Berlin Consul:

APPLICATION FOR THE ISSUANCE OF A VISA UNDER THE GERMAN QUOTA FOR FELIX FRÜHAUF, HIS DAUGHTER HELGA, HIS SON RUDOLF MAX, AND HIS MOTHER-IN-LAW LINA SCHWERIN. WAITING LIST NUMBER: 47,591 /A/B/C/

Dear Sirs:
With reference to records already on file:
I must inform you that my wife Mrs. Johanna Frühauf died in the United States as an American citizen. I have been told that consequently I may apply for visas only on the ordinary quota, but I hope that on the basis of my own and my children's registration dates the quota visas can be granted immediately. In the meantime I have received new documents from America in support of my application. I have been told that these documents were first submitted to Washington in support of my wife's application and that their return was requested after her death. I refer first of all to the affidavit by my uncle Meyer Vomberg and that of his [son] Arthur J. Vomberg. These affidavits show that our relatives are obviously well-off, established American citizens who, together with my aunt, possess assets in the six figures. The [documents] also show that my uncle is not only a well-to-do businessman, but also direc-

tor of the savings bank there. In this regard, I refer you especially to the enclosed letter[s] from attorney Bang and the Eaton Savings Bank.

May I point out that both these affidavits guarantee support only for me. However, I also enclose a statement from the Eaton County Savings Bank confirming that my uncle deposited the amount of $3,000, not only for my use but also for my daughter Helga, my son Rudolf, and my mother-in-law, and stipulating that this amount is to be paid to me in equal installments over a period of two years, provided that I arrive by January 1, 1941.

I have been informed that my uncle will arrange for the bank to extend this deadline. In any case, this shows that my uncle and my cousin know that I intend to emigrate to the United States with my family and that they are ready to provide for all of us. The omission of the names of my children and mother-in-law was a simple oversight, and since the files were sent to Washington in a great hurry, the additional change was not made.

Moreover, I am enclosing an affidavit from my brother-in-law Monroe Schwerin. I should also like to mention that, according to my late wife, my uncle and cousin looked after her in the most thoughtful manner and also expressed to her their interest in us. Not only did they put up the deposit of $3,000 . . . but they also generously arranged the financing of our trip to the United States.

I understand that they expect us in Charlotte, Michigan, immediately after our arrival in the United States and that they will put us up in their own home there. According to all the reports I have heard, I am convinced that with such support I will very soon be able to earn a living for myself and my family in the United States. In fact, I hope and expect that this will be possible without the use of the funds they have so generously made available to us . . .

Dr. Moses asked for a copy of Felix's letter to the American consul in Berlin and wished him much success.

Back on Track

On November 17, 1940, there was a letter from Felix's brother-in-law in Sheboygan:

Meanwhile we have received the news from New York that the affidavit matter is back on track. According to Herta and the lawyer, we first have to receive notification from the State Department; meanwhile this has arrived, and we think that now all the papers are already on the way to Berlin. . . .

Meyer Vomberg wrote on November 25:

> . . . am renewing the deposit to October 1, 1941. As soon as this is done I will send you copies. I hope that you and the children are well, as is the case with us. . . .

And on December 7th he wrote:

> . . . Enclosed find copy of deposit which I sent off to the American Consul in Berlin today—This deposit is valid until October 1, 1941. . . .

On December 5, 1940, Moses was able to submit an additional affidavit. It probably originated with acquaintances to whom Hilde had turned the previous spring.

> . . . Mr. and Mrs. Heinecke have said they are ready to make out affidavits for the entire family. Enclosed I am sending you the affidavit prepared in April with an additional one dated November 20 in which they extend the guarantee of support to include you and your son and daughter. . . .

Major Packing

Now preparations for the move shifted into high gear. On January 9, 1941, the packers arrived. They worked for three days—up to eleven hours a day. The bored officials sent by the Main Customs Office to supervise the packing passed the time playing a tabletop bowling game that the family wasn't allowed to take along. Absorbed in their game, they did not notice the Meiningen packers (bribed with a tip) secretly slipping silverware that they had hidden in their overalls during a sandwich break into the crates. When the packers completed their job, the customs collectors officially certified that they had discovered "no legal tender, securities (stocks or bonds), gold or precious metals, or any other articles subject to export duties or not allowed to be exported." They then sealed the lift with four lead customs seals—T84. The Customs Office collected 102.40 marks for this official transaction; the shippers charged 367.00 marks for the lift and 282.50 marks for handling, which included freight charges (see documents 18–20).

Because it was wartime, the emigrants' property could no longer be forwarded to Amsterdam for shipping; therefore, it stayed in Meiningen, where it was confiscated by the Finance Office in 1942 and expropriated.

Eluding Ghettoization

Early in 1939, after the Frühaufs finally made up their minds to turn their backs on Germany, they sold their house and property to an Aryan with the provision that they would have the right to live there until their departure. The buyer agreed but did not pay a penny for the acquired property.

Now, at the beginning of 1941, a new disaster threatened. The Nazis in Meiningen, as elsewhere in Germany, were getting ready to ghettoize the Jews, cramming them all into one building called the "Judenburg." To escape this coercive measure, Felix fled to Berlin with his children. There, in Pension Werres, Augsburger Strasse 37, they found lodgings with people who were not anti-Semitic. This place turned out to be very cheap for them, primarily because Helga helped in managing the pension. Felix wrote that he felt "at home" there, that the people were "likable and pleasant. Every evening the man of the house takes me along to have a glass of beer."

Forced Labor

In the spring of 1941 all Jews were assigned to forced labor. Helga had to work in an armaments plant, and Rudolf worked in the tannery of a leather factory. That meant twelve hours a day of hard work for each of them. Felix, who was suffering from a stomach ailment, was exempted from such toil. But he had the agonizing task of composing telegrams and letters, of constantly running to "Italcit" (the official Italian Travel Agency that transmitted and received telegrams), and of standing in line at Lloyd's, at the U.S. Consulate, and in the offices of emigration and foreign currency advisers. Again and again he had to go back to Meiningen to take care of personal matters or petty administrative affairs, such as obtaining certificates of good conduct. These forms always had to be made out in triplicate by two different citizens (not relatives), and they had to be notarized. Moreover, the good conduct certificates had to be made out anew every four weeks (see documents 21–24).

Ship Passages Are Booked and Accommodations Reserved: New Documents Required

On January 28, 1941, Dr. Moses, the lawyer in New York, acknowledged receipt of Felix's letter of November 27, 1940, which had taken two months to reach him, and wrote:

> . . . 1. Indications are that you should now be able to obtain quota numbers for yourself and your family.
> 2. Mr. Vomberg has informed me that on January 11 he asked American Express Co. to let the Consul in Berlin know by airmail that money for the ship tickets was deposited for you and how much.
> 3. Under these circumstances, I do not consider it necessary for you to go to another transit country temporarily; I think that you will be able to obtain American visas in Berlin.
> 4. You will not get preferential treatment because your wife was an American citizen. . . .

The American Express office in Berlin confirmed on February 15, 1941, that the $1,110 cost for the family' passage from Lisbon to New York had been paid (see document 25).

Given this situation, the news reaching them on February 25, 1941, that their documents had expired came as a terrible blow. After all, Felix had submitted the four affidavits as recently as November 27, 1940, and January 13, 1941, had handed in the certificate for the deposit of $3,000 on December 6, 1940, and as required had submitted a certificate confirming the booking of passages from Lisbon to New York on January 10, 1941. And American Export Lines, already holding $1,650 for the passages, was asking for the visas so that they could deliver the ship tickets! Up to that point the requirement of U.S. authorities had been: First, show us your ship reservations, then you'll get the visas.

Felix's letter of March 26, 1941, to the U.S. Consulate in Berlin laid bare the entire tangled mess and the total confusion of bureaucratic red tape: The delay had been caused by a mix-up of their applications and registration numbers. The Frühauf papers had not been filed under Helga's number, 47,591 a/b/c, but instead under Felix's number, 60,119. He was even asked to submit an application for form 633 (nonquota)—*after* the death of his wife (see document 26). Once again, they needed new papers.

Again the Frühaufs turned to their rich uncle, and Meyer Vomberg replied on April 2, 1941, writing while he was on vacation:

> . . . I received your letter of March 8th this morning. I am sorry that your trip here has again been postponed . . . I had not heard that your visas were denied because the time had expired. I can't make out new papers here, but I will write to Arthur today to start the ball rolling on new visa papers. . . . Do you have a plan for how you can use the $200 I sent you?
> . . .

On April 11, 1941, Vomberg wrote to tell them:

> . . . places for you from Lisbon for August 8 . . . I think you are putting more value on the things you want to take with you than coming here yourself. I think it would be better if you went to Lisbon and came to New York where you have relatives who can help you. . . .

And on April 19 Vomberg wrote: "New visas enclosed; [they] have also been sent to the Consul via air mail. . . ." (see documents 27–28).

At Last a Glimmer of Hope!

On May 7, 1941, the Frühaufs received official notice of the registration numbers assigned to Helga, Felix, and Rudolf, along with a request to appear at the American Consulate on June 26, 1941, between 10 A.M. and 12 noon to undergo physical examinations and to pick up their visas. This was the news they had been waiting for; once more their goal had come within reach. But they had to hand in the confirmation of their booked passages immediately: "the photocopy sent on April 21st this year by American Export Lines is not sufficient to meet the local requirements because it does not show that the booking is actually confirmed."

Their personal belongings were to be sent to Lisbon by air freight via Rome and Madrid with the help of an acquaintance, the export manager for Lufthansa, a Mr. Fuchs. But the boxes from Meiningen (containing linens, rugs, and a lot of other things) were too big for the airplane. In addition, they were supposed to be watertight. So, on May 9 they were repacked by two packers from Schmiedecke Forwarders, who lined ten wooden boxes with oiled paper and painted the outsides with reddish brown waterproof paint. They packed everything that would fit into twelve suitcases and one bedding bag and stowed these in the ten wooden boxes. That cost another 532 marks; the air freight charges for 1,410 kilograms (3,103 pounds) amounted to 7,350 marks, including shipping, transportation charges to the airport, and two months' storage charges (see documents 29–31).

Ten days later, on May 19, the affidavits Uncle Meyer Vomberg had promised arrived by airmail at the Berlin Consulate (see documents 32–33). Felix thanked him on June 10:

Dear Uncle Meyer,

. . . many thanks for the new papers which arrived promptly three weeks ago. As I wrote you on May 9th, I don't know whether they were necessary. The main thing is that we finally have been summoned [to the consulate] and I think we will be able to leave in four weeks; perhaps we can even take an earlier ship in Lisbon. I have to go back to Meiningen again in order to take care of the last formalities that are necessary before emigrating. . . . Last week, after the money was transferred from here back to New York, I sent [you] a cable asking you if you would transfer the $200 to Markus & Hartin in Lisbon. Whatever I don't need, I will immediately return to you once we arrive; also, I won't need the deposit; we want to work and earn our own living, which will not be difficult considering my children's experience and know-how.

You say you are concerned that the things I want to take with me won't be much use; believe me, dear uncle, I have given this careful consideration, and once [I] am there, [you] will say I was right. I'll be able to convince you of that as soon as we arrive. Most of the things belonged to Hilde, and with the help of the lawyer [I] will then set everything in order. . . .

This will probably be the last letter I will be able to write to you from here. If you want to write to me, you can send information to me in Lisbon c/o Export Lines from the middle of July on. Well, dear Uncle Meyer, thank you again, also on behalf of my children, for the great kindness and support you have bestowed on our emigration. I hope to be able to pay you back sooner than you expect. . . . Warm regards from your eternally grateful nephew Felix.

America Breaks Off Diplomatic Relations: No More Visas!

On June 22, 1941, German troops invaded Russia. As a result, the United States suspended diplomatic relations with Germany four days later. It was one of the blackest days for the Frühauf family. When they reached the American Consulate in Berlin at the prescribed hour the morning of June 26 to pick up their visas (see documents 34–35), they found themselves standing in front of a locked door. A porter opened it, saying, "The consulate was closed at 12 midnight. No more visas are being issued. The Swiss Consulate is acting as U.S. representative." Was this the end of the line for them?

❁

A Third Attempt

But should they give up now, having gotten this far with so much trouble and effort, and—according to a report from the shipping agent—now that a part of their baggage was already in Madrid? The Frühaufs were not ready to admit defeat. Even if everything else failed, they ought to be able to enter the United States through Cuba.

This route—going to the Unitd States by way of another country—was difficult and expensive. The Central and South American countries were constantly changing their laws and regulations or temporarily closing their borders to emigrating Jews. Their consulates were often poorly informed and worked very slowly; employees frequently took bribes for documents that were not quite in order. Even though these countries were ordinarily used by immigrants merely as a springboard to the United States, they demanded horrendous amounts of foreign currency. Cuba insisted that those who entered the country must show that they had as much as $1,500 to spend when they got there, and Cuban authorities imposed a fee of $50 to make sure that no person would become a burden to the state even during an intermediate stay.

Now in mid-1941, after the closing of the U.S. Consulate, there was a sudden run on Cuba. Between September and November 1941, about 35,000 visas were issued, but since there were not enough ships to take all the refugees to Cuba, they crowded into Barcelona and Lisbon.

And in Berlin, Felix once more hurried to Italcit on Unter den Linden to send his telegram messages, which were translated and transmitted "via Transradio"; then he had to run back to pick up the replies from America.

Calls for Help across the Atlantic

On July 3, 1941, Felix renewed his request to his uncle, which was followed on July 12 by a telegram to the lawyer Moses reinforcing his plea: FINANCE CUBA TRIP FRÜHAUF—URGENT—PERHAPS WITH REFUND [OF] DECEMBER DEPOSIT.

Felix's sister Martha cabled from New York: MEYER REFUSES PAY $750 PER PERSON—HERTA SHOULD TRY PERSUADE UNCLE.

The uncle's answer to Berlin: IN REPLY TO QUESTION OF JULY 3RD CANNOT ARRANGE FRÜHAUF.

On July 19 Martha was able to report: EVERYTHING ON TRACK—SPOKE VOMBERG PERSONALLY—PROMISES TO ARRANGE.

In the meantime, in a registered letter that went via Rome and Rio de Janeiro, Felix called on Dr. Moses in New York for help:

Dear Sir:

You are probably surprised to still be receiving mail from me from here. Unfortunately there was a mix-up with our papers at the consulate; with great difficulty [I] succeeded in getting an appointment to receive our visas for the end of June, and on that very day they stopped issuing visas.

In the meantime I have been in touch with Uncle Meyer by telegraph to ask him to make a deposit of $3,000 for Cuba for me and my two children as well as for my sister Recha here in Berlin. Just recently [I] received a cable saying that he refuses to do so. Today I sent him a telegram suggesting that he could use the $3,000 deposit that was made in the U.S. for this purpose if this is legally acceptable. It is the only emigration possibility left to us!

I would like to ask you, dear sir, to help me with this emigration; the matter is very urgent. My sister, Mrs. Joachimsthal, c/o Shulman, 793 14th Avenue, Paterson, New Jersey, or her daughter Herta Lehrer can give you the exact state of affairs with regard to the spending money for Cuba, since Mrs. Lehrer intends to visit my uncle in Charlotte, Michigan, in any case in order to arrange it all; or perhaps my sister has in the meantime somehow raised the money from acquaintances.

If our emigration to Cuba were to become possible, [I]

would send you a cable and you could immediately arrange in Washington for our immigration from Cuba to the U.S., so that we would not have to stay too long in Cuba.

Again I ask you most respectfully to do all this and to get in touch with my sister. (In any case, she can be reached by telephone since she works for Shulman.)

It is our last chance. . . .

Leaving No Stone Unturned

On July 23, 1941, Felix wrote to his sister Martha and his niece Herta:

. . . in case Cuba doesn't work out, I have initiated something else. That is, going via Switzerland, and perhaps [I] could get our visas for the U.S. there. If this were to work out, we three would need only $800; we have the passage tickets. Compared with this, Cuba costs much more, especially since the trip there costs about $600 per person in addition to the cash we need to have on entering. But then we couldn't take Recha with us, and I don't want to do that. If we can go to Cuba, then we already have tickets to New York and we would only have to pay an additional $200 to $250 per person, plus the entire fare for Recha.

The [departure of the] ship on which we booked passage from Lisbon has been postponed to August 20th, and I hope that everything will be all right by then. Again, there is only one thing [I] would again like to ask of you: do everything with the utmost urgency, that is the important thing. Ten days ago I wrote to Mr. Moses, the lawyer, and in the meantime he will have gotten in touch with you. Please discuss my new idea of immigrating from Europe with him. These days one has to try everything. I am sure you have already heard that a Form B is going to be issued by the visa office of the State Department in Washington. It can be filled out by you or by an official, or Moses ought to ask in Washington whether we could not get a visa from another (European) country since we were asked to come for a visa on June 26th, under No. 47,591 for Helga, No. 60,119 for me, and No. 65,261 for Rudi. But according to the registration dated September 20, 1939, we are all listed under number 47,591/a/b/c, and it was this double entry of our numbers that caused the delay. . . .

I think it is probably advisable that Uncle [Meyer] submit a request to Washington asking that they issue us a visa for the U.S. in Spain or Portugal; that way [I] would not need anything else, and we would have to arrange only for Recha to go to Cuba. I hope that we'll finally have some luck with this and that we will see each other again very soon. If we go to Cuba, [I] will have my baggage sent only as far as New York. To whom should it be delivered there? Please let me know. . . .

Three days later, another letter from Felix:

. . . Recha just telephoned; she has to pack up her things once again, this time by August 15th. It's a good thing that she rented a room back then. But I hope that by then Cuba will be all set. The Home is being broken up, and it is therefore uncertain where Recha will go after that. . . . The ball has been set in motion for the transit visas via Switzerland for me, Helga, and Rudi, and possibly we will get the visas very quickly. Then we would immediately go to Zurich, and a lawyer in Zurich would get us the visas for the U.S. This would cost about $500, and then [we] still need money for the trip to Lisbon, amounting to $300, so that makes $800 altogether. Should that work out, we can forget about Cuba for us and use it only for Recha. If we get out through Switzerland, it will save money because for us three the trip [to Cuba] costs around $750 more, that would mean a loss of $300, plus whatever we would need in Cuba. . . .

I hope our emigration will finally work out all right. It has become very urgent. . . . [I] would have gone immediately to Cuba if [I] had known of Hilde's illness. . . . As soon as we leave here, you can register us at the *Kongresshaus*. We could perhaps also go to Brooklyn since Walter lives there. But these should be the least of our worries. What matters is just to get out!...

Don't leave any stone unturned so that we can at last reach our goal. It is impossible to live here anymore—Gustav ought to be able to help, too. . . .

I am greatly puzzled that the April 1940 documents did not arrive until December!—That is another reason for our delay, and now let's do everything with the greatest haste. . . .

If we go to Cuba and make port in New York, please find out whether it would not be possible for us to be allowed to get off in New York. In that case Gus Friesner or Arthur would have to be there. . . .

These words reflect Felix's utter despair that, in spite of all their effort and trouble, nothing had so far been accomplished. Their hope to be able to board the *Exeter* in Lisbon on August 20 was fading fast.

Uncle Meyer wrote on August 4, 1941, with regard to their leaving for Cuba:

Dear Felix,
I received the cable, asking me to send $750 per person, which you would repay when you leave Cuba. In the first place, I don't have much faith that this will ever happen. Second, I don't have the money right now. Third, you also wanted to take Recha along (which pleases me as much as it does you), only I think she would be an obstacle to your coming to America. Once you are here, we can work on getting Recha out, too. I will do everything possible to help your emigration
. . . .

If it was difficult to obtain all the required documents, it was a near miracle to coordinate them for one fixed emigration date. Again and again some deadline expired, or a document, such as a character reference, had to be extended, or an endorsement had to be changed.

On August 4 Felix telegraphed his uncle: CUBA VERY URGENT—TRANSFER DEPOSIT TO BANK—WIRE REPLY TO US—ACCORDING NEW REGULATIONS FROM WASHINGTON CONTINUING TRIP TO NORTH AMERICA POSSIBLE ONLY IF [WE] TAKE RECHA. And to his sister Martha he

cabled: SURPRISED AT QUESTIONS—WHY NOT BETTER INFORMED—
CAN GO THERE ONLY IF TAKE RECHA ALONG—CUBA MUST BE
ARRANGED IN 8 DAYS—RECHA NEW ADDRESS AGAIN ON FIFTEENTH—
CANNOT OTHERS HELP—REQUIRES IMMEDIATE INTENSIVE PROCESS-
ING—OTHERWISE DONT DO IT.

Who Else Could Help?

Felix now turned to his most distant relatives. On August 15, 1941, he
wired to PULZER IN HAVANA/CUBA—FOR FELIX FRÜHAUF. The mes-
sage read: WIDOWED, SON RUDOLF SINGLE, DAUGHTER HELGA SINGLE,
SISTER RECHA SINGLE, ALL GERMAN CITIZENS, RESIDING BERLIN,
AUGSBURGER STRASSE 37/II, HAVE SPOKEN TO UNCLE MEYER VOMBERG,
CHARLOTTE, MICHIGAN REGARDING TOURIST STAY STOP CONTACT
VOMBERG IMMEDIATELY TO MAKE SEPTEMBER DEPARTURE POSSIBLE
STOP REQUEST CABLE REPLY.

He asked his sister Martha to involve her employer: HAVE NOT
RECEIVED NEWS ABOUT CUBA—TRY GET SHULMAN'S HELP SINCE NO
RISK.

And on August 18, 1941, he wrote:

Dear Uncle Meyer,
. . . I am very sorry that I have to keep turning to you. I have
really been having the worst luck with our emigration; you can
imagine how I feel. I have tried all possible ways to get out,
and now, because of the latest regulations from Washington of
which you have probably by now been informed, there is only
one way left for us: to immigrate to the United States via
Cuba. Unfortunately, when Herta saw you, she had not yet
found out about these regulations in New York so that she
could not tell you the exact details when she visited you. If she
had, we would be gone from here already because gaining
entry to Cuba is very easy once the money has been deposited.
Then [we] could leave within 14 days.

You think that you won't get your money back. That is not
the case, for I cannot and must not claim it. It will remain as
security, and once we leave Cuba, it will be returned to you

immediately. In Cuba $100 per person will be deducted to pay the lawyer; besides you can use the deposit from last December for that. . . .

Please find out, dear Uncle, whether it would not be possible, once we have the visa for Cuba and [the boat] docks in New York, whether it can be arranged that we can [get off and] stay there [in New York]. Perhaps that would require sending a request to Washington. I have also written to Herta about this . . . .

I would not burden you with this, dear Uncle Meyer, but there is no one else to whom I can turn who would process everything as thoroughly as you and who would find out about everything in such detail. I recognized this from the fact that Arthur went especially to Detroit on our behalf. . . . I promise that everything you spend for me will be returned to you. . . . I always admire your prudent forethought, dear uncle, and I can very well understand why you have such a respected position in the state of Michigan. Today I can only express to you our thanks for your great kindness; once we are over there, we will reciprocate in other ways. . . .

Our baggage is already in Madrid. We still have no confirmation of our ship reservations, but we have asked to be rebooked. . . . Tomorrow I intend to discuss everything again with my [emigration] adviser, and then I will perhaps send you a cable, because it takes too long by mail. Again, thank you very much. Warmest regards also to Aunt Mary and Arthur, Your nephew, Felix.

The Frühaufs received confirmation from Lisbon that $1,476 had been paid to American Export Lines for three ship tickets on the *Excalibur* leaving January 2, 1942. But no additional money was available to pay for the baggage.

"Only One Possibility Is Left: Cuba!"

On August 25, 1941, Felix turned to Martha:

. . . Recha is now at Derflinger Strasse 17. We're not sure for how long . . . . Haven't you inquired about the new immigration regulations? You must have known about these as long ago as the middle of June. Besides that, you should have immediately initiated [visas for] Cuba over there after [I] informed you by telegram that [I] did not get the visa. If you had done that, we would already be gone from here, perhaps we'd even be in Cuba by now. Some of our relatives, as soon as they found out that the consulate here was no longer issuing visas, immediately initiated Cuba over there and they have been gone a long time already. And now one can't get any more Cuban visas here!

As soon as [I] find out that the deposit has been made, I will try to get visas in Madrid. Didn't you try to find out whether, on the basis of our [earlier] notification to appear at the American Consulate, we could get our visas in Madrid, because now all those whose visas have expired are going to Madrid. . . . People who initiated Cuba at the same time we did left three weeks ago already. . . .

Above all, I hope to be able to take Rudi along. Indeed, there are always other worries. . . . Our baggage—12 suitcases, 10 boxes, 1 bag of bedding—is in Madrid. It all went on Lufthansa. I wish I were there. . . . Things are very difficult to arrange with Switzerland, because from Switzerland I would get only one U.S. visa, provided we all leave Europe. And then new documents would have to be filled out, as I wrote you on July 23. . . . Only one possibility exists: *Cuba*! Please find out and submit a request to Washington or the Joint [American Jewish Joint Distribution Committee] immediately for us to receive a visa in Madrid on the basis of our summons on June 26th [to the U.S. Consulate]. The Joint Distribution Committee also was able to arrange things with expired visas, and [I] suspect that they would also do it for those who had previously been summoned [to the Consulate to receive visas]. . . .

I beg you to make every effort so that things will at last work out. It is doubtful, as I just found out, that [I] will be able to take Helga along. There are constantly new worries. With warmest regards, Felix.

In October 1941, a secret decree issued by the Reich Main Security Office barred further Jewish emigration "for the duration of the war."

In the middle of September 1941 the Frühaufs found out that there was one chance left to fly from Munich to Spain on Lufthansa. And so they went to Munich, going to the airline office every day to ask for plane tickets. On September 20 this hope was shattered, too. Lufthansa informed them that the airline could no longer fly Jews out of the country. To get back to Berlin they had to have a special police permit because a decree, issued on September 1, required that, as of September 15, every Jew from the age of six up must wear a yellow star sewn on his or her clothes—and the Frühaufs were not yet branded like this. Now there was no hope left.

And Still They Don't Give Up

Once again telegrams chased each other back and forth across the Atlantic. Felix pleaded with his sister Martha and his niece Herta to save the family. Since Martha was only able to scrape together the money to pay for the expensive trip, he asked that they get the uncle to cable money to Switzerland and to make a deposit in Cuba for Aunt Recha. It was of the utmost urgency that the Cuba visa be issued for Felix within the next few days—or he would no longer be able to get out.

On October 6, 1941, he cabled Meyer Vomberg and Herta Lehrer: EMIGRATION VIA SWITZERLAND SPAIN POSSIBLE IF [YOU] WIRE 300 DOLLARS TO AMEXCO BASEL.

On October 26 there was news from New York: SEND URGENT CABLE—ASK VOMBERG MAKE DEPOSIT FOR RECHA—WE PROVIDE CUBA PASSAGE—REPLY TO US—JOACHIMSTHAL.

The following day Berlin telegraphed Martha Joachimsthal: FELIX EMIGRATION POSSIBLE ONLY IF CUBA VISA ISSUED THIS WEEK IN BERLIN—TELEGRAPH REPLY IMMEDIATELY. The reply came from New York on October 29: FRÜHAUF CUBA EMIGRATION IN PROCESS—CABLE VOMBERG AGAIN.

And on November 3, 1941, Vomberg wired: CABLE DETAILS WHAT FRÜHAUF WANTS ME TO DO—RECHA WILL BE OBSTACLE.

Ghettoization

In the fall of 1941 a Nazi order declared that Aryans in Berlin could no longer "be expected" to live in the proximity of Jews. The Frühauf family had to leave Pension Werres and was moved into the eight-room apartment of the Sommerfelds, a Jewish family who lived on the third floor at Rankestrasse 27a. Together with their fellow Jews—each room housed a different family—they managed to scrape by. On October 22, 1941, in a letter written from the new address, Felix complained:

> My dear ones, For two months now we have received no letters from you at all. (The last news was August 8). . . . Why did you not complete the Cuba [application]? It could have been done three times over between July and today; it took other people from 2 to 3 weeks to get it done completely. It can't be Uncle's fault since he has done everything I asked; the important thing is, he must be given all the details. . . . If you want to see Recha again, then arrange Cuba!
>
> I cannot understand that my telegram of August 8th did not give you sufficient information, and why [I] received no answer to it. Letters are no use at all, only cables [go through]. This is no time for chatty letters, only for action. I spent almost [all] my money, and I now have Dominican visas, for the children too, but the Hilfsverein won't put us on its list because of the children. For that reason I am trying Switzerland/Spain and am now waiting only for a French transit visa. Then we can leave immediately. But just as a precaution, arrange Cuba for me. . . .
>
> One thing I have to repeat: Find out all the details, then it will work out. If I were over there, Gustav [Felix's brother] would no longer be here, and above all Recha wouldn't be here anymore. I doubt that we will ever all be reunited again!—You don't seem to be worried about this. Haven't you heard what is happening here!?
>
> I went to Munich with the children in the middle of September so that we could fly to Spain. On September 20th it was no longer possible to do that. Now we are pinning our hopes on Switzerland, otherwise the children won't be able to [get out]; that is why you should arrange Cuba for me, so that I can get out and so I can then help the children [to get out]. Dear Martha, please leave your pots on the stove and arrange Cuba urgently!
> Warmest regards, Felix.

Frühauf's lament, "I don't know whether I can take Helga and Rudolf along," was based on a "Secret Order" to the Reich Organization of Jews in Germany decreeing that the emigration of any Jews under the age of sixty "is not possible at this time." A short while before that, they said that old people were an obstacle to the immigration process, especially handicapped people like Felix's sister Recha, who had a deformity. On the other hand, emigrants were not allowed to leave close relatives behind in Europe. There was no escape from this vicious circle.

Felix gave up. He had moved heaven and earth—all to no avail. He could no longer go on.

Now it was Helga's turn to take over, to plead with the uncle. For, even though the Frühaufs had visas for the Dominican Republic, Honduras, and Spain, they still lacked transit visas for Switzerland and unoccupied France. Felix could have made it to Spain with a Hilfsverein transport, but he had to have a Cuban visa for that, otherwise they wouldn't put him on their list.

Grasping at Straws

The Frühaufs thought that once Felix made it to Spain, Helga and Rudolf could follow. So Helga sent an imploring letter to the uncle:

BERLIN, OCTOBER 28, 1941

Dear Uncle Meyer and Aunt Mary,
You will probably be surprised that I'm writing to you today. But Daddy has put the entire emigration matter in my hands, and so I know more about these things than he does. Therefore I am writing to you in order to give you a detailed report. First thank you, also in Daddy's behalf, for the money that you made available to us in Basel. We will need that money when we arrive in Basel, God willing, and when we go from there to Spain. All three of us have visas. Daddy has a San Dominican visa; Rudolf and I each have a Honduran visa. As a result of that we also got Spanish visas. As soon as we arrive in Spain, we think and hope that, on the basis of our call-up to the American Consulate on June 26, 1941, we will get [U.S.] visas.

Four weeks ago we planned to fly to Spain. We were already in Munich, but unfortunately it was no longer possible.

Three weeks ago I applied for a visa for us three at the Swiss Consulate, and I am now waiting for the final word from them. At the same time I also applied for French visas, since one has to go to Switzerland via France. I hope to hear this week what will become of us. If the route via Switzerland does not work out, then Rudi and I can't get out.

I therefore ask you, dear Uncle, to immediately arrange the Cuba visa for Daddy so that at least he can get out to Spain with the Hilfsverein transport. Then he can stay in Spain until we get there. The Hilfsverein will not assign Daddy to the transport on the basis of his Dominican visa alone. That is why he needs the Cuban visa, too. I hope that in the meantime you have already arranged the Cuba visa for Daddy. I hope that you will stand by us in these difficult times and that you won't desert us, or we will never see the grave of our dear Mama.

We would like Daddy to leave now because it is more likely that he can help us from Spain rather than here. Thank God we can both take care of ourselves if Daddy should no longer be here, and perhaps we could join him there even sooner than if he were to continue to stay here with us.

But if indeed everything goes wrong and we can't emigrate any more, then you can claim our baggage which is already in Madrid (Spain) through the firm of Baquerre, Kusche & Martin (there are 23 pieces of luggage). Daddy has already informed the company.

Dear Uncle Meyer, please do what I ask as quickly as possible. You have no idea how upset and worried we now are. Please don't delay under any circumstances, or everything will be too late. Daddy must get out, otherwise Rudolf and I will be desolate and lost. And Aunt Recha, too, needs a Cuba visa immediately. . . .

By the beginning of November not all the baggage had arrived in Spain. When Felix inquired as to its whereabouts, Lufthansa informed him that a "freight traffic jam" especially in Munich had caused the delay. The boxes marked FF [Felix Frühauf] 29/30, which were shipped from Berlin to Munich on August 7, 1941, remained in Munich until October 23 and were then shipped from Rome to Madrid on October 30. The boxes marked FF 21–24 were transported to Munich on August 19, stored there until October 15, then forwarded to Rome, and they left Rome on November 10 via Madrid. The bag of bedding was shipped from Berlin to Munich on August 19, and from there on October 17 to Rome and finally, on November 3, to Spain.

Once Again Close to the Goal

On December 2, 1941, Meyer Vomberg telegraphed from America that the Frühaufs' entry into Cuba had been approved that Friday—the entry permit number was 31,293—and that the consul in Berlin was being informed of this. On December 6, Felix was given a certificate by the French delegation in Wiesbaden permitting his transit through France. On December 23 the Spanish Consulate in Berlin confirmed that the visas issued to Helga, Rudolf, and Felix Frühauf were still valid and that they had the right to enter Spain.

That same day Felix was asked to appear at the Swiss legation within the next few days with regard to his entry into Switzerland:

Your entry permit for a stay in Switzerland has come in. You must present to us your valid German passports with the exit visas, also valid entry visas for overseas states, ship tickets for passage from a Spanish port, and valid Spanish and French transit visas all entered in your passports, the former giving the right for a short stay in Spain. You must enter [Switzerland] before February 5, 1942 via Basel.

The $300 required for transit through Switzerland and Spain were on deposit at the American Express Company in Basel. And as required, $1,476 for the ship tickets had been paid to American Export Lines in Lisbon.

Yet by February 3, 1942, the passports with the exit visas had not been returned to Felix by the head of the district administration in

CONSULADO DE ESPAÑA
EN
BERLIN

Berlin W 15, den 22.12.41
Bleibtreustr.27

Bescheinigung

Es wird hierdurch bescheinigt, dass die Visa Nr. 5410, Nr.5411 und Nr.5276, welche vom hiesigen Konsulat an Herrn Rudolf Fruehauf, Frl.Helga Fruehauf und Herrn Felix Fruehauf noch Gueltigkeit haben und zur Einreise nach Spanien berechtigen.

Der Spanische Konsul

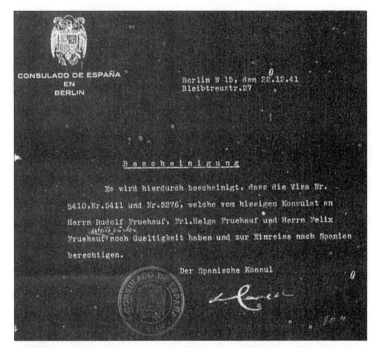

FIGURE 13 Confirmation from the Spanish Consulate in Berlin, dated December 22, 1941, that the transit visas issued to Helga, Rudolf, and Felix Frühauf were still valid.

SCHWEIZERISCHE GESANDTSCHAFT
IN DEUTSCHLAND

Visa-Stelle im Haus der Schweiz
BERLIN NW 40
FÜRST-BISMARCK-STRASSE 4 22. Dezember 1941

K VI/E 5/13 148
Bitte in der Antwort dieses Zeichen anzugeben

Herrn Felix F r ü h a u f

B e r l i n W.

Rankestr. 27 a, II

Mit Gegenwärtigem bitten wir Sie, in Ihrer Einreise-Angelegenheit an einem der nächsten Wochentage in der Zeit zwischen 10-12Uhr auf der Gesandtschaft vorzusprechen.

Hochachtungsvoll
SCHWEIZERISCHE GESANDTSCHAFT
i. A.
Der Vicekonsul:

PS.
Ihre Einreisebewilligung für einen Aufenthalt in der Schweiz liegt hier vor. Sie wollen uns Ihre gültigen deutschen Pässe mit den Ausreisesichtvermerken, ferner den gültigen Einreisevisa überseeischer Staaten, Schiffspassagen ab spanischem Hafen, und gültige in den Pässen eingetragenen spanischen und französischen Transitvisa, die ersteren mit Berechtigung zu kurzem Aufenthalt in Spanien, vorlegen. Die Einreise hat vor dem 5. Februar 1942 über Basel zu erfolgen.

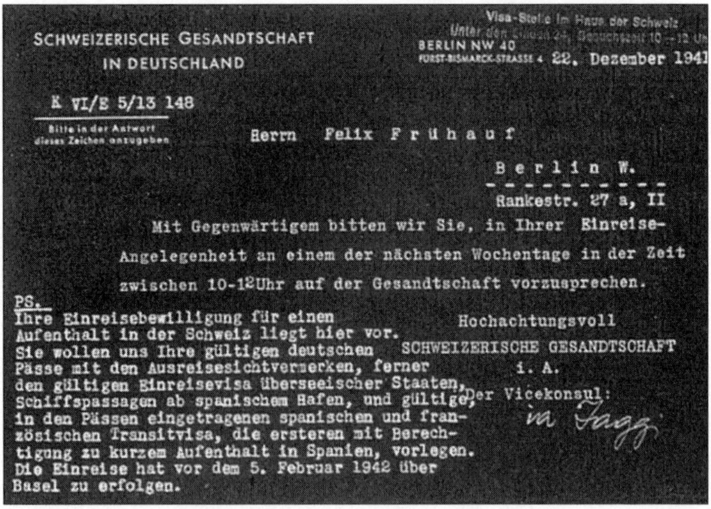

FIGURE 14 A letter to Felix Frühauf from the Swiss Legation in Berlin, dated December 22, 1941, with reference to obtaining transit visas.

Meiningen; consequently he had to ask for an extension from the Swiss Consulate. And as late as March 31, 1942, the Frühauf passports were still on ice at the Meiningen district administrator's office. Again Felix had to turn to the Swiss Legation and beg "most humbly" for an extension of the Cuban visa.

Once again it had all been in vain.

All Hope Is Lost

On December 11, 1941, Germany and Italy declared war on the United States. It was the end of the world for the Frühaufs.

Since the beginning of World War II in the fall of 1939, overseas mail service had been extremely undependable, and letters were frequently lost. A letter from North German Lloyd testifies to this:

> . . . Mail connections to and from America via Siberia take from three to four months, and with airmail one must reckon with theft of the mail. . . .

Once Germany declared war on America, direct contact with relatives in the United States was completely cut off.

The Frühaufs spent an immense amount of money for "emigration matters" that year. Their foreign exchange adviser in Berlin, Dr. Ernst Israel Aschner, submitted a bill amounting to 1,676.95 marks, primarily for cable costs as well as fees paid to the travel agency and Lufthansa. His own agreed-upon fee was 500 marks. These sums were deducted in regular prepayments from Frühauf's blocked account, number 25,864. In March 1941 Felix had credited to this blocked account the money in his savings account in the Verbandssparkasse in Meiningen—17,226.09 marks (see document 36). Helga's and Rudolf's wages were also deposited to this account. They never laid their hands on a penny of it.

The family subsisted on a monthly sum of 410 marks, fixed by the authorities in Rudolstadt on September 29, 1939. Because everything cost more in the big city, Felix applied in May 1941 for an increase in the family allowance of 150 marks. But as Helga remembers it, they were granted only 50 additional marks. Any expenditures above that amount had to be approved, and proof had to be furnished that the amount had been withdrawn from the blocked account.

On February 13, 1942, the foreign exchange office of the Regional Office of the Finance Ministry in Rudolstadt informed Felix that—based on the Law Securing [Blocking] Jewish Property dated August 16, 1939—his monthly tax-free allowance had been set henceforth at 250 marks. No reason was given for this reduction. In any case, Felix asked for an increase on February 26, 1942. However, the letters written by the exchange office show that they "asked" him to explain why he had not informed them, as required by law, of his move to a new residence and why he had not yet notified the police in Meiningen of his change of address. He made up for that immediately on February 26, 1942 (see documents 37–39).

Forced Labor in an Armaments Plant

Helga was conscripted to do forced labor in the F. W. Butzke engineering works. She was lucky at least in that her workplace was more than seven kilometers from where she lived. Consequently, she was permitted to use public transportation and thus avoided the long daily walk back and forth. That was worth a lot in those frigid wartime winters. Of course, as a Jewish woman, she had to stand during the ride on the streetcar.

The first thing one saw on entering the factory building was a sign in big letters: CAUTION! DO NOT ENTER! JEWS WORKING HERE! Together with about eighteen other Jewish women and two men, Helga toiled away at piecework either on the early shift from 6 A.M. to 6 P.M. or the late shift from 12 noon to 12 midnight. The Jewish Community delivered a scanty meal to the workers in the lunchroom.

Apparently only the four foremen and the boss knew what was being produced at F. W. Butzke, probably airplane or weapons parts. Helga worked at a turret lathe and made disks; they were a sort of metal plate, into which grooves were cut or ground. A foreman checked the measurements and, if necessary, ground them a little more. During every shift Helga had to finish at least seventy-two pieces. The disks were then put on a cart, wheeled outside, and packed into cases.

The foremen behaved typically. When the boss was in the room, they goaded the women and threatened them with the Gestapo: "If you don't do what you're told or make a mistake, I'll report you!" Once the boss had left, they behaved somewhat more moderately. Notwithstanding, conditions were brutal; twice Helga had a nervous breakdown. The first time she was confined to bed for six weeks, although she was repeatedly summoned to see the medical examiner.

The First Deportations

Early in the summer of 1942 a new batch of forced laborers arrived: some ragged, down-at-the-heel Polish women. Helga had to train one of these so-called Eastern workers. In the process she became infested with lice. Her head was crawling with them—they were almost impossible to get rid of! The dreadful itching nearly drove her crazy. On top of that, the hygienic conditions in the factory were miserable. And always there was the tugging fear, "Once the Polish women have learned the ropes, are they going to replace us, and will we then be deported?"

The first Jews were already being taken away from the factory. A rumor spread that they had been shipped to a labor camp. The only camp Helga knew about was Birkenau, because a Meiningen classmate had written her from there; but she hadn't said a word about what actually was going on in the camp. Still, you wondered what sort of torment awaited you if you were ever taken there.

Soon Aunt Recha also received an order to get ready for deportation. Helga went to visit the distraught woman to console and comfort her and to help her pack. She had been ordered to take two sets of clothes, a coat, a wool blanket, a cup, knife, fork, and spoon, and enough food for two days. When they parted, Recha said, "If you hadn't come, I would have killed myself!"

Signs of Compassion

Once, just after Helga had left the factory, an air-raid alarm sounded, and an air-raid warden pulled her into a cellar, even though Jews were forbidden to enter public bunkers and air-raid shelters. Another night, as she was on her way home, a stranger pressed a ration card for white bread into Helga's hand; the name on the card had been erased.

Her brother Rudolf had similar experiences. Over a period of several weeks a road construction worker would wait for him at a certain street corner and slip him a little package containing bread, meat, or fruit; sometimes there were cigarettes or even chocolate.

But Helga's greatest support in this dire situation came from her old friend Käthe Hauschild, the army officer's wife. Every week she would send a food package to a predetermined cover address in Berlin.

Again Too Late

In mid-1942—who knows through what roundabout ways—Felix found a man, a rather shady character, who, in exchange for a steep fee, went to Wiesbaden on behalf of the Frühaufs, who were not allowed to travel anymore. There he took their passports to the mission of the Vichy regime in order to get them visas for unoccupied France. There was very little time left. The extensions in their passports were due to expire on July 8, 1942. The courier was supposed to come back by train the evening before July 8 or sometime during that night. The next morning the Frühaufs would pick up their visas at the Swiss Consulate, and by 12 noon they would have started out for Zurich on the only daily Swiss Air flight (Jews were no longer allowed to fly on German airplanes). They waited in vain. The messenger arrived at 4:00 P.M. on July 8—four hours after the plane had left! At midnight their passports expired. All that money thrown out the window.

But perhaps the dates in the passports could be altered? It was really quite simple. You only had to put a number 1 in front of the 8 (in the date 8 Juli 1942). The Frühaufs actually did "correct" the date (see figs. 15a and 15b), but their fear that the forgery would be discovered was so great that they did not dare take the chance.

With that, their very last opportunity to leave the country was dashed. On August 20, 1941, the *Exeter* had left Lisbon without them. Half a year later, on January 2, 1942, the *Excalibur* had sailed

FIGURE 15A Passport (first page) made out to Rudolf Max Israel Frühauf containing a *J*
stamped into it on July 19, 1939. A state requirement identified passport holders as Jews
through the *J* and the added names Israel for men and Sara for women.

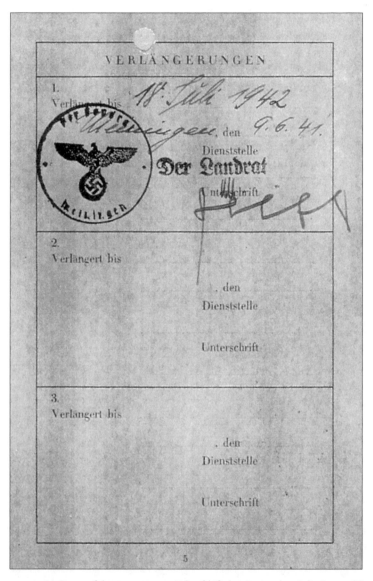

FIGURE 15B Page 5 of the same passport with a falsified expiration date: July 18, 1942 (18 Juli 1942); a 1 has been inserted before the 8.

without them. Their baggage was in Madrid. And *they* were caught in Hitler's Germany.

What else was in store for them? It is difficult today to imagine the mental and spiritual anguish the Frühaufs endured in those days. To have to eke out a bare existence, ostracized like lepers, the ever present danger, the shock every time one heard that this or that person had been picked up, the constant all-consuming fear about when their own turn would come! Then on top of that, there were the long hours of hard work Helga and Rudolf were forced to do, day in and day out.

❄

Fleeing the Bloodhounds

Several times while Helga was working at her turret lathe, the safety device on the machine would be triggered and the lathe would stop. The foreman would have to come over to get it going again. Eventually she discovered that she could easily cause the stoppage herself. One day, tired and despairing, she was mindlessly and monotonously turning her discs, when once again the safety device was activated. The foreman, who had become quite suspicious by then, yelled at Helga and assigned her to another work station. Then he inspected the lathe thoroughly to find out whether she had manipulated something.

At home, as Helga was telling her family about this ominous incident on the sixth day of January 1943, she was met with a fresh batch of bad news: Felix had been ordered to report to the Gestapo again! That set off the alarm. They realized that it was high time to disappear. All through the night they discussed what they could do and where they could hide. Helga didn't dare to go back to the factory; rather, she immediately went to see a Jewish colleague she had met at work who was married to a non-Jew. What, she asked the woman, was happening at the factory? Her coworker said, "They're in an uproar. You're wanted for sabotage, Helga. The Gestapo already has your photograph. If they catch you, they'll shoot you or arrest you on the spot."

Going into Hiding

Where could the Frühaufs go in this hopeless situation? They couldn't expect other Jews to conceal them—that would have unnecessarily endangered more lives—so they decided to seek shelter with

79

Aryan acquaintances who had the courage to help Jews. Quickly they gathered together some bare essentials. Felix hid with the shoe-maker across the way on Rankestrasse. Rudolf spent the night there, too—under the counter. For two weeks Helga changed her hiding place almost daily.

They stayed in touch through an address used as a cover. Finally, Helga went to a public phone booth to call Frankfurt am Main and plead with her girlfriend Luise Marx to take her in. Luise, a Chris-tian, was married to a Jew who, after having been imprisoned by the Nazis for quite some time in 1933, had emigrated.

Helga's brother managed to get an *Abmeldung* for Helga from a friend who was a graphic artist. This document canceled residence registration with the Berlin Police for the seamstress Helene Fröh-lich, born in Breslau, religious denomination Protestant, and last residence Berlin NW 87, Altonaer Strasse 15, tenant of Mrs. Eichner. They chose the name Helene Fröhlich because the initials H. F. were the same as those on Helga's linens and underwear, and they picked Fröhlich, which means "cheerful," because the times were so sad.

Once again Fuchs, the Lufthansa export manager, helped out. He took Helga—who of course was no longer wearing the yellow star—to the train station. And because he thought she would not be sufficiently safe in a regular compartment when the inspectors came through, he used his Lufthansa identification card to obtain a berth in a sleeping car for his "niece." But even after that, there were more dangers to overcome. Before the train left, all passengers had to line up outside the cars for inspection of their papers. Helga, who only had her police *Abmeldung*, felt more than queasy. But a word of assurance to the inspectors from the export manager worked. Miss Fröhlich did not have to present her identification papers. A jovial inspector even let her be the first to climb aboard. Relieved, she set-tled into her berth.

A Change of Identity

In Frankfurt am Main the next morning, Helga asked for directions to Luise Marx's apartment on Solmsstrasse. Once there, she used all her resourcefulness, carefully proceeding with the plan they had hatched in Berlin to save her life. First she changed her appearance; she colored her hair red and had new passport photos made at Poly-foto on the Kaiserstrasse. One thing was clear, she had to get out of Germany as quickly as possible. She had only a single lead: the address of a friend she had met in dance class, Peter Löwenthal, who lived in Brussels. Peter, who had been her sweetheart, had fled to Belgium some time ago; he had sent her letters through the most amazing and unlikely channels and had promised to marry her.

However, to cross the border she needed a passport, or at the least an International Postal Identification Card. She figured out how to obtain one. Her father was to send a registered letter to her at the Solmsstrasse address on a daily basis so that the mail carrier would get to know her. For several days the letters arrived. Then one day, Helga asked the mail carrier, a woman, not to deliver any registered mail for two days because she was planning to go on a hike with Mrs. Marx.

The next time the letter carrier came to the door, Helga told her with feigned dismay that she had lost her identity card while hiking in the Taunus Mountains the day before. They had been playing and running around in the woods with the dog, she said, and suddenly she realized that she didn't have her wallet any more. They searched for hours until it got dark but couldn't find it. And now she needed an International Postal Identification Card as a substitute. Could she get that at the post office? It was urgent because she was about to leave on a trip to Aachen.

"Of course," the mail carrier replied, "but bring along a passport photo."

Helga felt a tremendous sense of relief; the clever plan, it seemed, would work. When she applied for the identification card at the post office, the clerk—as expected—asked for someone who could confirm her identity. Helga suggested the letter carrier, who testified that she knew Miss Fröhlich who lived on Solmsstrasse. Helga paid 50 pfennig for the document, which would have cost 5,000 marks on the black market.

She intended to cross the Belgian border near Aachen and began to look for a suitable place from which to start out. After asking around for quite a while, the woman from whom her friend Luise bought milk gave her the address of a family named Mueller in

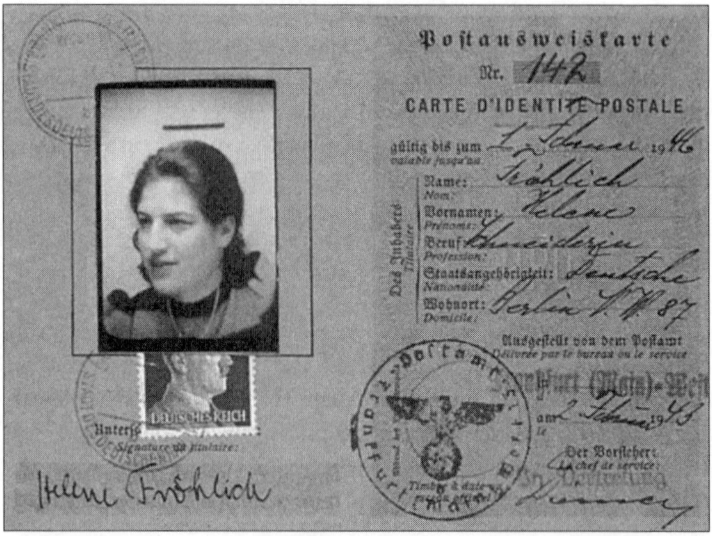

FIGURE 16 Identity card of the World Postal Organization (*Carte d'Identité Postale*, or International Postal Identity Card) made out by the German Reich Post Office on February 2, 1943, for Helga Frühauf, alias Helene Fröhlich, German national, born December 19, 1920, in Breslau, reddish blond hair.

Brand rote Erde (now called simply Brand) near Aachen. The Muellers would surely help her.

Helga left Frankfurt on February 2, 1943. Mueller, a soldier who was stationed on the eastern front but who happened to be home on leave, inquired in great detail about the reason for her trip. Helga dished up a touching fairy tale: Her seriously wounded fiancé lay near death in the main hospital in Brussels. He kept asking for her, and she absolutely had to see him just one last time before he died. Unfortunately, she had no entry permit for Belgium.

Mueller told her that the military command post in Aachen was responsible for such things. She went there. But even though she stepped forward with a snappy "Heil Hitler" and wore a conspicuous Winter Relief insignia in her lapel, she was turned down. "A wife or a mother, yes; but a fiancée, no," they said tersely. So she had to return to Brand without having achieved anything.

At that time—Mueller was already on his way back to the Russian front—the news reports from Stalingrad were coming in. Weeping women from the neighborhood, worried about their husbands and sons, gathered in the Muellers' living room trying to comfort one another. Helga stayed with Mrs. Mueller a few more days; she helped her with the laundry and ironing and cared for the children. On Sunday Mrs. Mueller took Helga along to the Protestant church service. In order to keep from being conspicuous, she said she was Catholic and allowed the children to explain the ritual to her.

A friend of Mrs. Mueller who was touched by Helga's story had a suggestion. She knew a woman who was the proprietor of a restaurant in Hombourg (in the Belgian District of Eupen). This woman went to Liège, Belgium, twice a week to get food supplies, and she always brought something back for her, too. Perhaps she would take Helga along with her across the border.

To Belgium as a "German Fiancée"

Helga took the next bus to Hombourg. She looked up the restaurant proprietress and told the woman her story. While they were talking, three soldiers entered the restaurant—a sergeant, a corporal, and, as it turned out, an engineer from a nearby V1 rocket launch site. There was a great to-do over Helga! A young woman in the one and only restaurant in this godforsaken dump was quite an event. "Where are you from?—Where are you going?" In no time at all, a lively conversation was under way. Helga once again charmingly rehashed her moving story: . . . and so she absolutely had to get to Brussels—if need be even without an entry permit.

"That's no problem; we drive across the border every day. We'll take you with us," the soldiers said. Helga almost threw her arms around their necks. She immediately went to get her suitcase and mailed the remaining food rationing cards and all her money—except for the ten marks one was allowed to take out of the country—to Mrs. Marx for her father.

When Helga returned to the restaurant that evening, she found it full of soldiers. But in the meantime, the sergeant got cold feet and backed out of his offer. He could take her suitcase, he said, but a woman in the car, that was too risky.

At that the corporal snapped to attention, "If you don't mind, sir, I'll walk across the border with Miss Fröhlich!" That was all right with the sergeant. So the corporal and Helga trudged off through the deep snow. First they climbed up a slope, then they walked along some railroad tracks. Helga's companion started nervously at every sound. He seemed to be more afraid than she. Suddenly he stopped. "I'd like to ask you a question," he said. "What are you going to do once your fiancé dies?"

"I'll go back to Berlin; after all, I have my work," she replied.

He told her that he was a food chemist and that he lived in Leipzig in his mother's house; his father was dead. "You can come live with us. Here is my address. Then, when the war is over, we'll get married. Maybe we can even marry before then. Will you promise me that you'll come to Leipzig?" Helga promised.

They continued along the tracks. After they had walked an hour and a half—it was close to midnight—the silhouettes of several houses emerged from the darkness; they had reached Aubel. They were in Belgium! A sentry, pointing his gun at them, asked for the password. "And who is the woman?"

"She's my fiancée," the corporal replied. They were allowed to pass. Helga's companion knocked at the first door they came to and asked for a room for his "fiancée." Two older women, intimidated by the sight of a German soldier, gave Helga their best room and treated her like a princess. The next morning they invited her to have coffee with them. But hardly had they taken their seats at the table when the three soldiers from the previous evening appeared, their arms loaded with rolls, butter, and jam. And so, they enjoyed an opulent breakfast together. At noontime, the three soldiers again dished up a meal. Helga felt freer than she had ever felt before—it was as though she had been reborn. She had made it!

Just then one of the women remarked out of the blue, "You know, Miss Fröhlich, you have such a lovely Jewish nose."

Helga flinched. "That's an unbelievable insult," she said, and began to complain about the Jews for all she was worth. The other woman tried to soothe her; good Lord, it wasn't meant that way— she really had such a lovely face. The corporal came to the defense of the Jews. He knew many Jews in Leipzig, he said, and they were all right.

Helga ended the macabre scene by saying, "Oh well, I've had some bad experiences with those people."

After supper, the sergeant bought Helga a train ticket, her "husband-to-be" gave her 300 Belgian francs, and the third soldier handed her a food package for the trip. Thus provided for, Helga went to Brussels in a fourth-class compartment. The date was February 10, 1943.

❀

From Hiding Place to Hiding Place:
Life as a Fugitive

She arrived in Brussels on a Wednesday. The stock exchange was open, it was market day, and the city was teeming with activity. German military police patrolled the streets and checked every suspicious-looking passerby. A soldier whom Helga asked for directions to Peter's house referred her to a nearby policeman and said, "If he doesn't understand German, smack him; then he'll understand."

She made her way to Rue van der Kindre and found the tobacco store Peter had described. But he wasn't there. Two women who owned the store told her he had had to go into hiding. They knew his new hiding place and they would send for him.

When Peter came, they embraced. But there was little time to express their joy at seeing each other again. The newly arrived fugitive had to be hidden as quickly as possible. Peter found a little room for Helga where she could stay temporarily, no more than fourteen days. She also had to earn money as soon as possible. And so Peter brought Helga to Madame Ida van Pelt, an elderly Jewish lady who earned a living by mending clothes and bed linens, turning shirt collars, and altering dresses. Helga helped Madame van Pelt with her sewing two or three times a week in exchange for a meal and a little money.

Madame van Pelt's name had been Ida Odenheimer; she was from Hamburg. After the death of her husband, Aunt Ida, as Helga soon called her, followed her son, who had emigrated earlier, to Belgium. When the Germans invaded Belgium, some resourceful refugees set up a marriage bureau for Jewish women who wanted to obtain Belgian citizenship. Mrs. Odenheimer, whose son and daughter-in-law had meanwhile gone on to Cuba, decided to enter into one of these sham marriages that would promise her safety. Jean Baptist van Pelt, a construction worker employed in Germany, was prepared to marry Ida for 5,000 francs. In order to scrape enough money together, she even had to sell her typewriter. After the civil marriage ceremony, they each went their own way. Every four weeks Mrs. van Pelt baked a cake, added some cigarettes and other things, and sent the package to her husband. He thanked her with letters, and so outward appearances were kept up. But one day, quite unexpectedly, Jean Baptist appeared at her door, having left Germany because he was afraid of the devastating air raids. He found work at the Etterbeck barracks but was killed fourteen days later during an Allied air raid. Now Madame Ida was a war widow. She received a pension and was invited to be a guest of honor at the festive unveiling of a memorial to the victims of that air raid.

In the Clutches of the Gestapo

Although Peter helped her in many ways, Helga soon came to realize that marrying him was out of the question. In his letters he had sworn eternal love, but either in spite of, or because of, the constant danger in which he lived, he plunged into one amorous adventure after another. At the time he seemed to be involved in a steady relationship with a waitress.

One day a friend of Peter's, extremely upset, came running in, "You have to disappear, Helga! They've picked up Peter." She was thunderstruck. Distraught, she hurried to Peter's parents who, in the past, had made it plain they didn't like her. The Löwenthals nearly fainted when they got the dreadful news. Hysterical with fear that Helga might have been followed and that she might have put the police on their trail, the parents asked the upset girl to leave. Seemingly forsaken by God and the world, Helga was once again without refuge.

In the days that followed, as Helga rushed from one place to another like a hunted animal, Peter's friend acted as her guardian angel. They met secretly after dark, and one day he said, "I found a place for you; you can sleep there one or two nights." Helga was glad to have a spot to sleep even if it was only in a bathtub. Whenever she couldn't find shelter, Aunt Ida took pity on her and let her stay for the night. In her search for sanctuary, Helga also spent one night with the family of a dentist named Fischer. Luckily, she did not sleep there the following night, but instead stayed with customers for whom she had been doing some sewing past curfew time. As she prepared to go back to the Fischers' the next evening, Peter's friend intercepted her just in time and said, "You can't go there; the Fischers were picked up last night!"

At Last a Roof Over Her Head

Aunt Ida, seeing Helga in such dire straits, introduced the desperate girl to a "mixed-marriage" couple named Schwarz; they in turn knew Martin Bader, a German Jew who was living completely isolated and alone in a house he had rented from a Belgian woman. He had fled Nuremberg in April 1933 after some Nazi rowdies descended on him and his friends while they were playing cards; there had been a terrible brawl, and he decided he had better go underground. Taking off for Switzerland, he eventually came to live in exile in Belgium.

When Helga was introduced to the reclusive Bader, he said he would be willing to take in the homeless young woman until he found a tenant who could pay rent. "After all, Miss Fröhlich, I can't ask *you* for money." Overjoyed, Helga ran to pick up her little suitcase. At last she had found a home for the foreseeable future—she felt safe again.

"Miss Fröhlich," Bader asked after she had moved in, "are you the young woman all the emigrants in Brussels are talking about? I heard that you succeeded in getting out of Berlin at the very last minute last February and that you then managed to make your way here. I simply couldn't believe it. I thought that the people who were telling the story were making it up."

"Yes, it's true," Helga conceded. "I'm the one."

The house on Rue Félix Delhasse 14 was an ideal hiding place. It was located between the headquarters of the German Army and the villa of Foreign Minister Spaak, which was guarded by the Belgian police. Bader knew the police officer in charge, and the officer had promised to alert Bader to any raid or roundup. In such a case Martin and Helga would have concealed themselves in a secret compartment under the stairs.

Getting provisions worked out, too. A Belgian named Matthieu, who worked in the Resistance, brought them food twice a week. The only things Helga had to buy herself in town were eggs and butter. These shopping trips were dangerous, for the Nazis struck without warning. On one occasion, military police stopped the streetcar she had taken, ordered the passengers out into the street, had them line up next to a wall, and then inspected and searched each person meticulously. Helga was terrified, and in her agitated state she dropped her gloves as she got off the streetcar. One of the policemen picked them up and asked the crowd of people to whom they belonged. Helga came forward and took her gloves back. When she saw that the first group of riders had passed inspection and were already climbing back aboard the forward car, she pretended that she was one of them, thus avoiding the police check. Still frightened, she got off after a few stops, preferring to walk the rest of the long way home.

Help from the Resistance

Helga had met a Belgian woman named Jeanne Descamp who worked for the Resistance. Soon the two became close friends. Jeanne often brought food to Helga, and through the Resistance she got her a forged worker's pass for the Belgian railway. It was made out to Hélène Fabry, born in Ath. The name and place of birth had been chosen because they were easy to pronounce and because German was spoken in that border district. In addition, Jeanne arranged for a second safe house in case the worst happened. "After all," she said, "you can't be sure that you won't have to get out of Bader's house some day."

It was also through Jeanne that Helga found out that Peter had been taken to the collection camp at Mechlin (Malines), a city in central Belgium. Helga was able to send eight packages to him there; she had to deliver them to a certain spot at the Gare du Midi, and from there they were forwarded to him. Helga also helped the Löwenthals send him two packages. And with Jeanne's help, a medical orderly smuggled out letters from Peter confirming that he had received the food packages. He asked Helga to put his things in a safe place and to sell his suits. Four weeks later Peter was sent to an extermination camp. Helga never heard from him again.

Life Goes On

Helga and Martin Bader, who was thirty-two years older than she, got along very well. With time they developed a deep affection for each other and decided to get married after the war. It seemed as though everything was going smoothly. But then in October 1943, as though the constant fear of being discovered weren't enough, Helga became seriously ill. She was paralyzed on one side, and it seemed the one man who could help her was a Dr. Herz.

Dr. Herz was from Jülich, a city in North Rhine-Westphalia. He had been an army doctor in Belgium during World War I. During the occupation of the Rhineland, he successfully treated high-ranking Belgian officers and government officials. In recognition of such meritorious service, King Albert of Belgium had offered him Belgian citizenship.

Now Dr. Herz had been ordered by the Gestapo to treat Jews who were supposed to be transported to concentration camps but who were too sick to go. What a cursed assignment: to make people well so that they could be murdered! Even when he succeeded in getting a Jew admitted to a hospital, it usually wasn't long before the victim was picked up and deported.

It just so happened that the fatuous and brutal head of the Gestapo in Brussels and Dr. Herz were both Rhinelanders. Using Rhineland humor and risqué jokes, the physician took advantage of their "regional bond" to buy the goodwill of this man who was master over life and death. Dr. Herz even succeeded in getting people out of the infamous Gestapo "cellar," including a friend of Bader's, Emil Schönmann.

Once three uniformed soldiers turned up at Dr. Herz's office and asked him to use his connections with the Gestapo to help free a young Jewish woman—let's call her Judith—who was serving a sentence in the cellar. From the start, something about these men seemed fishy to Dr. Herz; he suspected a trap. So he said there was no way he could possibly do anything. At that point the three men dropped their disguise; they weren't German soldiers but, rather, members of the Resistance. The young Jewish woman was the fiancée of a pilot in the Royal Air Force. The men asked Dr. Herz to do everything he could to get her out of there.

At his next meeting with the Gestapo chief, Dr. Herz launched into a veritable barrage of jokes and anecdotes. Finally he came out with his request.

"Out of the question!" was the reply. Nothing could be done; Judith had to stay in the cellar. Dr. Herz pulled out all the stops. Suddenly the Nazi poked him amiably in the side, "Tell me, are you pestering me so much because she's your girlfriend?"

Dr. Herz stammered in embarrassment and finally replied, "You really notice everything, don't you?"

The next day Judith was set free.

Dr. Herz also saved Helga. In October 1943 he secretly went to Bader's house and cured her neuroparalysis. In the spring of 1944 he again made a dangerous house call to treat Helga for a serious abdominal problem.

❀

Arrival of the Allies: Liberated at Last!

During the night of Sunday, September 3, 1944, Helga and Martin were startled out of their sleep by noises coming from the German Army Headquarters. Evidently there was great confusion next door. They could hear orders being shouted, a lot of running back and forth, and much yelling. Trucks, some of them marked with the Red Cross insignia, drove up, were hastily loaded, and roared off with screeching tires. Piles of papers were going up in flames.

In the morning the picture became clear. The Germans were leaving Brussels, helter-skelter, without a fight. Shortly before noon, Helga saw the last German soldier depart, a poor exhausted fellow dragging his tired nag behind him.

The citizens of Brussels could hardly believe that peace had arrived. The news raced through the city like wildfire: The Germans are gone! Helga and Martin Bader couldn't grasp it! All the horror was behind them now—at last they were really free! They ran into the street, Helga supporting Martin, who for twenty-five months hadn't taken a step outside his front door.

Brussels was a sea of flags. Belgian, French, British, and American flags hung out of windows to greet the Allied troops as they entered the city. People were wild with joy. Nobody seemed to be afraid that the enemy would return. Helga and Martin walked down Avenue Bruckmann to find the Schwarz family.

But now a new infernal dance began: a pogrom in reverse. The Resistance stormed apartments belonging to Rexists, the Belgian Nazis; they beat and arrested the men, and drove them, their heads shaved, their hands raised above their heads, through the streets. Their belongings were tossed into the gutters and torched. Walking through Brussels was like tackling an obstacle course.

One Belgian woman said mockingly that the Germans had left so quickly, the whores had no time to wash before the Allies arrived. A British brigadier whom Martin and Helga met told them that at German Army Headquarters they had come upon a locked room; inside was a German soldier, drunk to the point of unconsciousness, lying among a heap of empty bottles. He was an army chaplain from Aachen, and he was celebrating the end of the war in his own way.

Other Signs Mark the Nazi Rout

Black market prices plummeted. Coffee, which had cost 5,000 Belgian francs before the liberation, was now practically being given away at 200 francs. Shop windows were filled with stockpiled and hoarded goods. It seemed as though everything was available again.

The previous summer Bader had had a serious argument with his landlady; it had upset him so much that he wanted to leave the house on the spot, even though he had paid rent for three years in advance. A few days after the liberation, on September 6, 1944, Helga and Martin moved into quarters Jeanne had obtained for them on Rue d'Anderlecht No. 41. The new apartment was very humble: one room, a kitchen, and a tiny storage room. The toilet was outside in the courtyard; one had to get water from a tap half a story up. But they were both happy. Jeanne helped them out with a few pieces of furniture and contributed pots and dishes. Helga made a closet out of egg crates. The war was not yet over, but they were able to get by.

Martin immediately volunteered his services to the Allies. Because of his fluent knowledge of French and English, he was much sought after as an interpreter. He wore a white star to identify himself, so that the Allied soldiers would know they could turn to him.

He used his legal expertise to help some Jewish acquaintances as well as others who had been cheated by Belgians to get their money back; for this effort he received a commission of 10 percent. For his friend Emil Schönmann, Bader was able to get back 10,000 francs from an antique dealer who had defrauded Schönmann. Since life was gradually getting back to normal and some job prospects for

Bader were beginning to emerge, the couple decided to remain in Belgium.

Helga Retrieves Her Identity

Once again there were bureaucratic hurdles to tackle. It turned out to be more difficult than expected for Hélène Fabry, alias Helene Fröhlich, to resume the identity of Helga Frühauf, the Jewish woman from Meiningen. First she had to be officially registered. Because the only proof of her real identity—the old German passport with the letter *J* and the names "Helga Sara"—had been stolen from her pocketbook, she tried to find witnesses who could testify to her true identity. Luckily, at the Jewish organization COREV (Comité Central Israélite pour la Réconstruction de la Vie Religieuse en Belgique/Central Committee for the Rebuilding of Jewish Life in Belgium) she met Günter Blitz, a former dance-class friend from Berlin. He was able to identify Helga. The Jewish Community also examined her thoroughly before they recognized and confirmed her as being Jewish.

A petty official at the Brussels residents' registration bureau, who had asked Helga to return the identification card she had been using up to that point, was going to make trouble for her because she had "misused" the name Fabry, which just happened to be the name of a relative of his. Finally she did receive an identity card, but with the stipulation that she report twice a week to the police and that she not leave Brussels. This nuisance continued for a year and a half—until May 1946.

"Mother of the Army"

On the eve of September 19, 1944, fourteen days after the liberation of Brussels, the Jews of the city celebrated their New Year. The synagogue couldn't hold all the people who attended, among them many American and Canadian soldiers. Therefore the Rue de la Rechence leading to the courthouse was closed to traffic, and the religious services were piped outside. After the ceremony, Martin and Helga

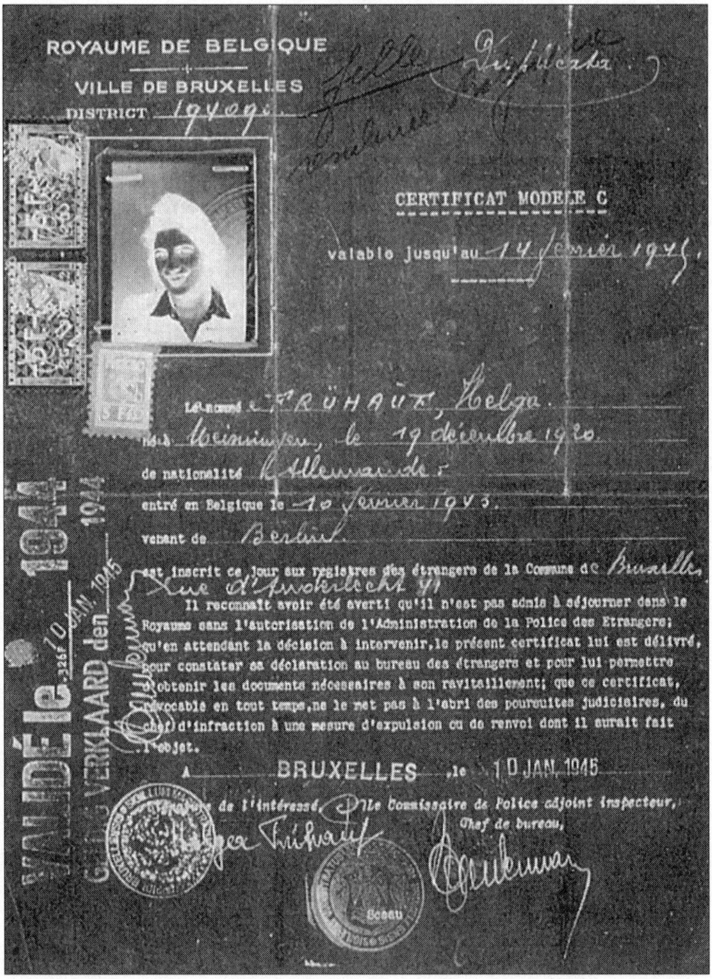
ROYAUME DE BELGIQUE

VILLE DE BRUXELLES

DISTRICT 19409

CERTIFICAT MODELE C

valable jusqu'au 14 février 1945.

Le nommé FRÜHAUF, Helga.

né à Meiningen, le 19 décembre 1920.

de nationalité Allemande.

entré en Belgique le 10 février 1943.

venant de Berlin

est inscrit ce jour aux registres des étrangers de la Commune de Bruxelles, Rue d'Anderlecht 41

Il reconnaît avoir été averti qu'il n'est pas admis à séjourner dans le Royaume sans l'autorisation de l'Administration de la Police des Etrangers; qu'en attendant la décision à intervenir, le présent certificat lui est délivré, pour constater sa déclaration au bureau des étrangers et pour lui permettre d'obtenir les documents nécessaires à son ravitaillement; que ce certificat, révocable en tout temps, ne le met pas à l'abri des poursuites judiciaires, du chef d'infraction à une mesure d'expulsion ou de renvoi dont il aurait fait l'objet.

A BRUXELLES, le 10 JAN. 1945

Signature de l'intéressé, Helga Frühauf

Le Commissaire de Police adjoint inspecteur, Chef de bureau,

VALIDÉ le 10 JAN. 1945

GELDIG VERKLAARD den 1944

FIGURE 17 Helga Frühauf was issued a Model C Certificate (Certificat Modele C) and was thus registered on the Belgian List of Foreigners. With her signature she acknowledged that the possession of this certificate did not entitle her to any legal rights. The document could be revoked at any time. The police branch that dealt with foreigners retained the right to promptly expel the holder of the certificate from the country in case she violated any laws. The document was important to Helga because she was able to get food ration cards by showing it.

spontaneously invited a strapping blond Canadian soldier and his two buddies to come to their apartment with them. In spite of the humble quarters, the soldiers immediately felt at home and enjoyed their meal.

In the meantime Helga had found some work to do at home. She sewed lace edging on handkerchiefs on which an artist had painted the famous buildings of Brussels—the castle, the marketplace, the courthouse, and the inevitable Manneken Pis (a famous fountain figure of a young boy urinating). She earned a decent amount doing this work. Things were looking up, and the couple kept an "open house." Soldiers of the Jewish Brigade of the British army, as well as Canadians and Americans, were constantly their guests. Twice a week Helga went to the fish market to buy green herrings, which she served in a variety of ways: as rollmops (a marinated herring filet wrapped around a gherkin or onion), fried, or as Bismarck herring. She also offered her guests kosher meat and cold cuts. Pretty soon Helga became known as "the mother of the army."

And then something really unexpected happened. As Helga came home one day, an American soldier was waiting for her outside the house. "Yes, you're the one," he said. "I know you from New York."

"Oh, I'm sorry," Helga replied. "I've never been to America in my life."

"That's not true," the soldier insisted. "Why are you lying?"

Bader came to her defense, protesting that Helga had never been in New York. He asked the soldier, "Are you Jewish? Come upstairs with us!"

"No, I won't go with you; your wife is a liar." But later he decided to accept their invitation after all. In the apartment, he stared at a photograph atop the radio. "You *were* in New York!"

"No, I was never there," answered Helga, "but if you mean the woman in the photograph whom I resemble a lot—that's my mother, and she did live in New York."

The solution to the puzzle was quite simple: the soldier had worked as a window cleaner in New York and lived with his grandmother right across from Hilde Frühauf's apartment on 47th Street. In 1939 he had seen Hilde almost every day.

"La Guerre est Finie!"

On May 8, 1945, Helga was helping her friend Jeanne clean up after her daughter Babette's communion party when suddenly there was a lot of noise and commotion on the street. Thousands of voices were shouting, "Finie, finie—la guerre est finie!" At last, the war was over.

The telephone rang. It was Martin; his voice breaking, he said, "Come to the Café Augustin, Helga. I'm heading over there with some friends."

The streetlamps were just going on as Helga elbowed her way through the euphoric, cheering, tumultuous crowds. In the middle of it all, overwhelmed by emotion, she began to weep like a little child. Not until a stranger asked her what the matter was did she pull herself together and continue on her way to the Augustin. There, everyone was in a state of wild excitement. Martin and his friends were celebrating the victory. They sang and drank and jumped up on the tables. It went on like that until dawn. On the way home they joined other exuberant people who were still dancing in the streets and in the squares. A half dozen friends came back to the Rue d'Anderlecht with them. Each brought something for breakfast. After they had eaten, they returned to the streets. For a week Martin and Helga hardly went to bed.

Martin, an experienced businessman, soon found work as a salesman for a raincoat company, and Helga worked at the same firm as a manager. Both made pretty good money for those times.

Threatened with Deportation

But in the spring of 1947 another disaster unexpectedly threatened them. As Helga was picking up their food ration cards, she was told to go to the police station. There, they confiscated her identity card and told her she would have to leave Belgium. Within twenty-four hours she was to present herself at a camp and from there would be sent back to Germany; she was allowed no more than 25 kilograms (55 pounds) of baggage. Helga was flabbergasted and ran to see her friend Jeanne, who said, "They must be mad. We'll just hide you again. You're not going back to Germany, no matter what!"

The reason behind this remarkable policy of the Belgian authorities quickly became clear: Many women who had followed the German Army were trying, with forged papers, to stay in Belgium. And Helga, as a German, was being lumped together with these women. The Belgian attitude was, "We've got enough prostitutes of our own; we don't need you."

This time the Jewish organization COREV was not able to help her; they suggested she go to the Mechlin Society (*Malineser Verein*), which was taking care of former inmates who had survived the concentration camp that once was located there. There were victims at the Mechlin camp who had not been transported to extermination camps because of the rapid advance of the Allies. When Helga called at the society's office, they told her that the man she was to see, a Mr. Vomberg, would not be available until that afternoon.

The mention of the name Vomberg electrified Helga. Her father's uncle in America, who had been so helpful, was named Meyer Vomberg, and her paternal grandmother's maiden name was Vomberg. After she had tried to figure out all the ways he could possibly be related to her, Martin, who had been listening in exasperation, griped, "Oh, don't bother me any more with all your relatives!"

That afternoon as Vomberg, an imposing man, entered the room where Helga was waiting, she thought, "He's the spitting image of my grandmother." She immediately asked him where he came from.

"From Belgium," he replied.

"And your ancestors?"

"They're from central Germany."

"Were they from Aschenhausen?"

"Yes."

"Do you have a cousin in Holland?"

"Yes, in Züpfen."

"And counting everybody, the whole family, parents, children, and grandchildren, are there forty of them altogether?"

"How do you know all that?"

"My grandmother was born a Vomberg!"

Vomberg jumped up, embraced Helga, and exulted, "I've found a cousin!"

It was easy for Vomberg, who had once been the Belgian consul in India, to cancel Helga's impending deportation. A brief talk with the Head of the Sûreté (the Belgian Security Police) was sufficient, and she was able to pick up her identification card at the Palais de Midi. What did she care about the sullen manner of the official who reluctantly handed her the document?

In the fall of 1947 the Baders were able to afford a new apartment and moved to Chaussée de Mons 348. There Helga was faced with a new inconvenience: The authorities withdrew her work permit. But by then she and Martin had become so much a part of the raincoat firm that she was able to continue working there without a permit.

❖

Searching for Traces

After the war, when the vast extent of the Nazi crimes was made public, Helga's uncertainty about the fate of her father and brother became unbearable. Regular mail service to Germany was reinstated after April 1, 1946, and it was once more possible to send letters. She wrote to all her relatives and friends. Käthe Hauschild, Reichenbacher the shoemaker, and Mrs. Thrän had survived the bad times in Meiningen. The house and property that had once belonged to the Frühaufs had not been damaged. But there was no indication as to what had happened to either her father or her brother, Rudolf.

Searching for traces, with the help of the Jewish Community in Berlin and the Missing Persons Tracing Service of the Red Cross in Arolsen, proved to be extremely difficult. According to information provided by the Jewish Community, Felix was deported to the extermination camp at Auschwitz on February 19, 1943, with the Twenty-ninth Eastern Transport (Osttransport) and died or was killed there toward the end of July 1943. But he was not listed in the Berlin Gestapo's transport list under that date. According to police documents, Felix Frühauf, prisoner number 4871, was transferred from the police jail in Frankfurt am Main to Berlin on August 2, 1943. He had probably been captured by the Gestapo while trying to hide in Frankfurt—he was believed to have been staying in the city as early as the spring of 1943, using forged papers that identified him as Gerhard Eichler. According to the Gestapo transport list, he was deported to Auschwitz with the Forty-first Eastern Transport on August 24, 1943. Rudolf was thought to have been part of the same transport. After that there was no trace of either man. The decision of the Berlin District Court, as communicated to Helga's lawyer, concluded with these words:

Under the circumstances, there can be no doubt of their deaths as a result of the extermination measures. Determining the exact dates of their death as you requested has been unsuccessful. Probable date of death can therefore only be established as May 8, 1945, the day the war ended. (See documents 40–44.)

Felix's brother Gustav, a teacher in Leipzig, who was two years older, and his wife, Ida, were deported to Theresienstadt on February 17, 1943. Their daughter, Änne, had been picked up ten days earlier and taken to the same camp. From there they were transported eastward. After that all traces of the family vanished and they were presumed dead.

Felix's younger sister, Recha Frühauf, was transported from Berlin to Riga, Latvia, in the summer of 1942. According to a death certificate issued by the Berlin Registry Office, she died there on July 20, 1942.

"There Must Be Another Suitcase in Berlin"

In the course of her investigations, Helga remembered that they had left a suitcase in Berlin containing school report cards, property deeds, emigration documents, and letters. As a favor to the Frühaufs, the helpful and courageous Lufthansa Export Manager Fuchs had agreed to retain it for safekeeping before they went into hiding. Since he was afraid at the time that the documents in the suitcase might be discovered in his house, Fuchs left them with a friend, the proprietor of the canteen at the Hermann Göring Barracks. As a result the documents were saved from destruction when the house where Fuchs lived was totally bombed out. Before the Red Army moved into Berlin, the manager of the airport assembled all his staff and told them that the last plane was leaving immediately for Flensburg and whoever wanted to leave had to board at once. Not wishing to leave his wife behind, Fuchs stayed and was given all the keys for the airport offices and storage facilities. After the plane had taken off, he unlocked the storage rooms and invited others who had also remained behind to grab whatever they could. He himself took food. On the way home he drove by the barracks. There, he warned the canteen proprietor, "The Russians are coming. You'd better get out of here as fast as you can. But first, please give me back my suitcase."

In May 1946 Helga asked a British army major to go to see Fuchs in Berlin and pick up the precious suitcase. He brought it back to Brussels, undamaged.

The search for the Frühaufs' other goods is a story in itself. The lift containing their furniture had never left Meiningen. In 1942 it was confiscated by the tax office and its contents sold. Helga was told there was no way to find out through official channels what prices the items brought and who had gotten rich thereby, although Münch, the shipping agent in Meiningen, made several efforts to find out. He eventually discovered that the tax office actually could have provided this information.

And what happened to the baggage that remained in Madrid? Helga remembered the name of the Spanish shipping company, and out of an old address book she dug up the address of the forwarders Bakumar, Baquerra, Kusche & Martin. It turned out that almost all their baggage had been lying in Madrid for the last five years—three boxes were lost, one suitcase was damaged, and one had been mended. The forwarders were ready to deliver the baggage for a payment of $600. When the National Bank in Brussels refused to send the money to Spain, Uncle Meyer Vomberg once again came to the rescue, transferring the money to Madrid.

He couldn't help remarking how many new things they could have bought for that amount! But for Helga it was not just the material worth; she wanted to preserve the memory of her parents' home.

The boxes, suitcases, and bag of bedding reached Brussels during Passover 1947. To everyone's delight, the linens and even the smuggled silverware and other items turned out to be undamaged. Just a few crystal bowls and vases were broken. On the other hand, all their woolens had been consumed by moths. Only the buttons were left.

❁

Return to Germany

It was with mixed feelings that Helga and Martin went back to Germany for the first time in July 1950. They wanted to clear up some property questions in Lüdenscheid and Mülheim on the Ruhr and to have the family graves restored. There were bureaucratic difficulties and legal problems, and they had to go back several times.

People in Lüdenscheid still clearly remembered the Schwerin grandparents and their prestigious clothing store. Again and again Helga was mistaken for Hilde Schwerin because of the amazing resemblance to her mother.

Martin liked being in his old homeland. He was impressed by how the people were tackling the postwar problems. He saw evidence of reconstruction and sensed a change of heart among the people. He kept saying, "It's our culture, after all." Helga, on the other hand, was in no hurry to return. She was still haunted by memories of what she had endured.

In June 1952 they decided to make a new start in Frankfurt am Main. An important consideration for them was that a Jewish community was again taking root in that city. They sent the following announcement to their friends:

Helga Frühauf and Martin Bader have the pleasure to announce that on June 21, 1952, they are legalizing their happy marriage* of nine years at the registry office here [in Frankfurt].

*During the years in Belgium they had lived as husband and wife, but without benefit of a legal ceremony.

Anyone who assumes that the German authorities would simply and without question recognize Helga Frühauf, a native-born German, as a German citizen knows nothing of the mysteries of bureaucracy. When she applied for an identity card at police headquarters, presenting her birth certificate, her father's birth certificate, and his army identification card, she was turned down. The reason given was: All Jews had been deprived of citizenship in the Third Reich, and therefore her status was that of a stateless person.

On the other hand, Martin, who had been expatriated by "special decree," had no difficulties. His German citizenship was acknowledged immediately. The district court even issued the couple a "certificate of marriageability" (Ehefähigkeitszeugnis) without any difficulty and at no charge.

When Helga subsequently went to police headquarters, an official there congratulated her, "Now you are a German citizen by marriage, Mrs. Bader."

But Helga was not content to leave it at that. She was German by birth and wanted to be recognized as such. Stubbornly she stood up for her rights, and finally, in October 1952, her German citizenship was restored "by order of the *Regierungspräsident* [District Commissioner] in Wiesbaden."

Martin Bader died on October 7, 1957.

Some months later, in the spring of 1958, Helga met K. A. Cohn, who had come to Frankfurt on a visit from Israel. He had fled from the Nazis in 1939, taking an adventurous and circuitous route through Hungary, Romania, and the Black Sea to reach Haifa.

On meeting Helga, he decided to stay in Frankfurt, and the couple were married on January 27, 1959. But after twenty harmonious years of marriage, Helga was widowed once again on January 1, 1981.

Through all those years she was active in the Jewish Community in Frankfurt, serving as chairwoman of the Frankfurt Society of Christians and Jews and on the board of directors of the Women's International Zionist Organization (WIZO).

Helga died on March 17, 1995; like her mother, Hilde, she died of cancer.

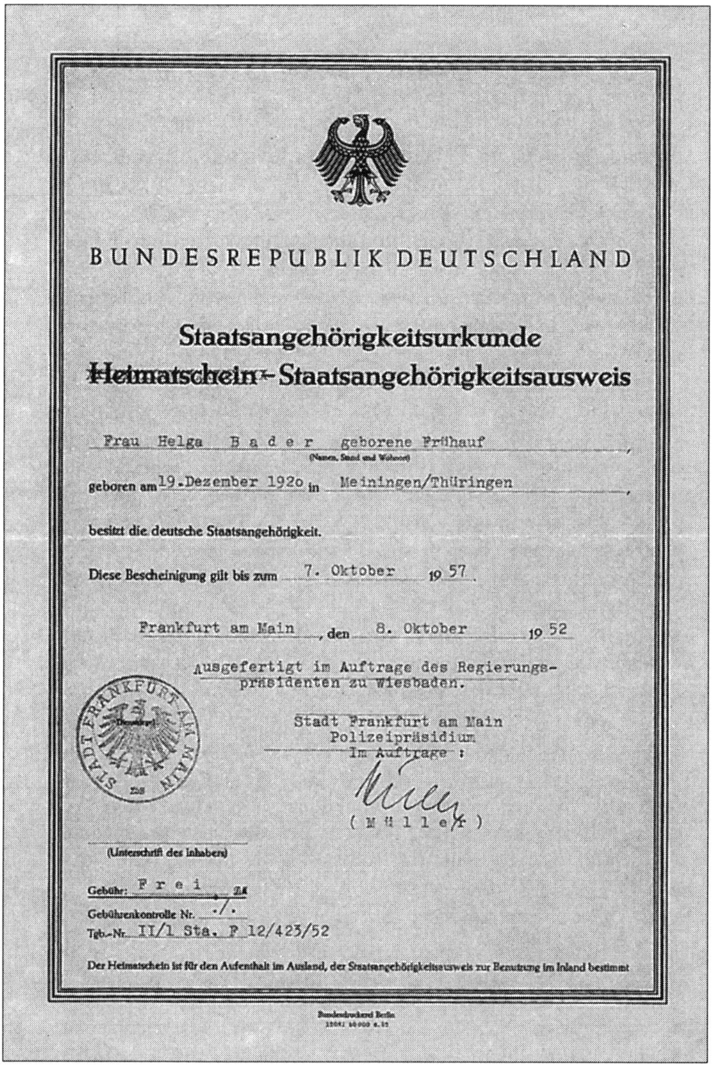

BUNDESREPUBLIK DEUTSCHLAND

Staatsangehörigkeitsurkunde

~~Heimatschein~~ - Staatsangehörigkeitsausweis

Frau Helga B a d e r geborene Frühauf,
(Namen, Stand und Wohnort)

geboren am 19. Dezember 1920 in Meiningen/Thüringen,

besitzt die deutsche Staatsangehörigkeit.

Diese Bescheinigung gilt bis zum 7. Oktober 1957.

Frankfurt am Main, den 8. Oktober 1952

Ausgefertigt im Auftrage des Regierungspräsidenten zu Wiesbaden.

STADT FRANKFURT AM MAIN

Stadt Frankfurt am Main
Polizeipräsidium
Im Auftrage:

(M ü l l e r)

(Unterschrift des Inhabers)

Gebühr: F r e i

Gebührenkontrolle Nr. ./.

Tgb.-Nr. II/1 Sta. P 12/423/52

Der Heimatschein ist für den Aufenthalt im Ausland, der Staatsangehörigkeitsausweis zur Benutzung im Inland bestimmt

Bundesdruckerei Berlin

FIGURE 18 Certificate of Citizenship of the Federal Republic of Germany made out to Helga Bader, née Frühauf, dated October 8, 1952. Helga had fought stubbornly to get this legal confirmation of her status.

✿

Documents

The application filed by the Frühaufs on May 9, 1940, for the return of the family jewelry and valuables was rejected (Doc. 1) on the grounds that Hilde Frühauf was not an American citizen at the time of her emigration. Therefore, after the August 27, 1940, expiration of the deadline for redeeming the valuables with foreign currency, the savings bank had to hand them over to the municipal pawnbroking institute in Berlin to be sold (Doc. 2). The sale occurred on January 8, 1941.

DOCUMENT I

Der Oberfinanzpräsident Thüringen
(Devisenstelle)

Herrn
Felix Israel Frühauf

Meiningen
Strasse der SA 18

Rudolstadt,
15. Mai 1940.

Schwarzburger Straße 60
Fernsprecher 5 22 und 5 25
Sprechzeit: nur 9–12 Uhr

Dev. / II J 10145 / l Tr / L.
[Bitte in jeder Zuschrift angeben]

Betr. Ihren Antrag vom 9. Mai 1940.
Hinterlegungsdepot für Gegenstände
aus Edelmetallen bei der Städtischen
Sparkasse in Meiningen.

Zurzeit der Auswanderung Ihrer Frau Johanna, gen. Hilde Frühauf, nach U.S.A. war dieselbe noch keine amerikanische Staatsbürgerin. Ich vermag aus diesem Grunde Ihrem Antrag auf ersatzlose Herausgabe der Ihrer Frau gehörenden Schmuckgegenstände nicht stattzugeben. Sofern Sie also Wert darauf legen, die Gegenstände nach U.S.A. an Ihre Frau nachzusenden, bleibt es nach wie vor bei meinem Vorbescheid vom 4. April 1939, d. h, die Gegenstände können nur dann freigegeben werden, wenn der in dem Gutachten bezeichnete Devisenbetrag an die Reichsbank abgeliefert worden ist. Um Ihnen dieses zu ermöglichen, verlängere ich hiermit noch einmal die Gültigkeitsdauer des obenangeführten Vorbescheides – Aktenzeichen: Dev. II J 10145 / 1 R /B – bis zum 31. Juli 1940.
Die depothaltende Bank braucht den ihr erteilten unwiderruflichen Auftrag, die nicht bis zum 15. November 1939 bzw. 15. Mai 1940 durch Devisenzahlung ausgelösten Gegenstände an eine öffentliche Ankaufsstelle zu veräussern, nicht vor dem 15. August 1940 auszuführen, sofern ihr der verlängerte Vorbescheid bis zum 31. Mai 1940 vorgelegt wird. Die durch § 1 der Dritten Anordnung aufgrund der Verordnung über die Anmeldung des Vermögens von Juden vom 21. Februar 1939 auferlegte Ablieferungspflicht wird insoweit mit Ermächtigung des Herrn Reichswirtschaftsministers ausgesetzt.

Im Auftrage
gez. Unterschrift

DOCUMENT 2

Verbandssparkasse Meiningen – Zella-Mehlis

MÜNDELSICHER

Herrn
Felix Israel Frühauf,

Meiningen
Strasse der SA 18

Hauptgeschäftsstelle Meiningen
Meiningen, den 27. Aug. 1940

Betreff: Verschlossenes Depot Nr. 886
Unter Bezugnahme auf das Ihnen von der Devisenstelle Rudolstadt zugegangene Schreiben vom 15. Mai d. J. ist die Frist für die Veräusserung der bei uns hinterlegten Gegenstände mit dem 15. August 1940 abgelaufen, nachdem Sie von der Möglichkeit einer Auslösung der Werte durch Zahlung in Devisen keinen Gebrauch gemacht haben.
Wir werden nunmehr der uns durch § 1 der Dritten Anordnung aufgrund der Verordnung über die Anmeldung des Vermögens von Juden vom 21. Februar 1939 auferlegten Ablieferungspflicht nachkommen und die in obigem Depot enthaltenen Werte an die
Städtische Pfandleihanstalt Abt. III – Zentralstelle –
Berlin NO. 55, Danzigerstrasse 64
zum Verkauf gelangen lassen.
Von dem Depot halten wir uns entlastet.

Verbandssparkasse
Meiningen – Zella-Mehlis
gez. Unterschriften

Order to Secure Jewish Property (*Sicherungsanordnung*), which in effect was meant to block all Jewish assets, served to Felix Frühauf by the Regional Office of the Finance Ministry on September 12, 1939 (Doc. 3). In paragraph 3, the order set an allowance (*Freibetrag*) of 200 marks for the Frühaufs, which was raised on September 29, 1939, to 410 marks after Felix Frühauf filed an appeal.

DOCUMENT 3 FOLLOWS

Der Oberfinanzpräsident Thüringen
Devisenstelle

Geschäftszeichen

J. S. 114   Sch/Fa.

Rudolstadt, ...9. September 1939
Straße der SA. Nr. 60
Fernruf 524

An

Herrn

Felix Israel Frühauf

Meiningen/Thür.

Mit Postzustellungsurkunde!

12. SEP 1939

aus 1879 bis ..
Staat. Sparkasse
...
...

Sicherungsanordnung

Um sicherzustellen, daß Sie Ihr Vermögen nur in Übereinstimmung mit den Devisenvorschriften verwerten, ordne ich auf Grund des § 59 des Devisengesetzes vom 12. Dez. 1938 (RGBl. I S. 1733) folgendes an:

I. Verfügungsbeschränkungen.

1. Sie haben binnen 5 Tagen nach Zustellung dieser Sicherungsanordnung

a) ein auf Ihren Namen lautendes und als

„beschränkt verfügbares Sicherungskonto"

zu bezeichnendes Konto bei einer Devisenbank — gegebenenfalls unter Verwendung eines bei einer solchen Bank bereits bestehenden Kontos zu errichten;

b) der Bank die beiliegende Abschrift dieser Sicherungsanordnung auszuhändigen;

c) die Bank zu veranlassen, mir die Errichtung des Kontos sowie die Aushändigung der Abschrift alsbald auf anliegendem Vordruck Dev. VI 3 Nr. 2 zu bescheinigen.

Das Sicherungskonto darf nur bei der Bank geführt werden, die die Abschrift der Sicherungsanordnung in Händen hat. Über das jeweilige Guthaben auf diesem Konto dürfen Sie — vorbehaltlich der Ziffern 3, 4 — nur mit schriftlicher Genehmigung der Devisenstelle verfügen.

2. Neben dem beschränkt verfügbaren Sicherungskonto dürfen Sie weitere, bereits bestehende Bank-, Sparkassen- und Postscheckkonten beibehalten, über die jeweiligen Guthaben auf diesen Konten jedoch nur durch Übertrag oder Überweisung auf Ihr beschränkt verfügbares Sicherungskonto verfügen.

3. Ohne Genehmigung dürfen Sie über das jeweilige Guthaben auf Ihrem beschränkt verfügbaren Sicherungskonto bis zu einem Freibetrage von vorläufig

RM. 200,—   (i. B. RM.   zweihundert

je Kalendermonat verfügen. Zwecks Prüfung der Angemessenheit des Freibetrages ist mir der anliegende Vordruck Dev. VI 3 Nr. 2 ausgefüllt einzureichen.

Vordruck Dev. VI 3 Nr. 1 (K 329)   28. 8. 39. 5000

4. Ohne Genehmigung dürfen Sie neben dem monatlichen Freibetrag über das jeweilige Guthaben auf Ihrem beschränkt verfügbaren Sicherungskonto für eigene Rechnung sowie für Rechnung Ihrer Ehefrau und Ihrer minderjährigen Kinder zu folgenden Zwecken verfügen:

a) zur Bezahlung und Sicherstellung von Steuern, Gebühren und anderen Abgaben, an Strafen und Auslagen an öffentliche Kassen und Notare;

b) zur Bezahlung von Beiträgen, Umlagen und anderen Abgaben an die jüdische Kultusgemeinde;

c) zu unentgeltlichen Zuwendungen an behördlich genehmigte soziale oder religiöse Einrichtungen;

d) zur Bezahlung von Anwaltsgebühren, ähnlichen Entgelten und Auslagen an Rechtswahrer, jüdische Konsulenten und Devisenberater für jüdische Auswanderer;

e) zur Bezahlung von Entgelten für ärztliche, zahnärztliche und tierärztliche Behandlung sowie von Krankenhaus-, Bestattungs- und Grabpflegekosten;

f) zu solchen Zahlungen, die zur Verwaltung Ihres inländischen Vermögens sowie des inländischen Vermögens Ihrer Ehefrau und Ihrer minderjährigen Kinder erforderlich sind;

g) zum Erwerb von Wertpapieren und Reichsschuldbuchforderungen, wenn der Ankauf durch Vermittlung der kontoführenden Devisenbank erfolgt;

h) zur Beschaffung von Sachen zum Zweck der Auswanderung (diese Sachen müssen bei der Auswanderung in dem Umzugsgutverzeichnis aufgeführt werden);

i) zur Bezahlung der durch die Auswanderung entstehenden Fahrtkosten, Transportkosten und Konsulatsgebühren;

k) zur Bezahlung anderer Schulden, sofern sie vor Zustellung dieser Sicherungsanordnung entstanden sind;

l) zur Bezahlung ersatzloser Abgaben und zur Veräußerung des Guthabens an die Deutsche Golddiskontbank.

Zahlungen der vorbezeichneten Art dürfen nur an Inländer und nur durch unmittelbare Überweisung seitens der kontoführenden Devisenbank an die Empfangsberechtigten geleistet werden. Sie dürfen nur auf Grund von Rechnungen oder sonstigen Belegen ausgeführt werden, die die Bank mit einem Zahlungsvermerk zu versehen hat. Sie haben alle derartigen Belege zur jederzeitigen Prüfung durch die Devisenstelle oder die Zollfahndungsstelle sorgfältig aufzubewahren.

II. Einzahlungspflicht.

1. Sie haben Bargeld und Schecks, die sich bei Zustellung dieser Sicherungsanordnung in Ihrem Besitz oder in Ihrer Verfügungsmacht befinden, sofort auf Ihr beschränkt verfügbares Sicherungskonto einzuzahlen.

2. In Zukunft dürfen Sie Zahlungen gleich welcher Art nicht mehr bar, sondern nur noch auf Ihrem beschränkt verfügbaren Sicherungskonto entgegennehmen.

3. Der Besitz von Barmitteln über den Freibetrag hinaus ist nicht statthaft.

III. Benachrichtigungspflicht.

1. Sie haben alle Banken, Sparkassen- und Postscheckämter, bei denen Sie zur Zeit weitere Konten unterhalten, und außerdem sämtliche anderen Personen, Versicherungsgesellschaften, Firmen usw., von denen Sie jetzt oder in Zukunft einmalige oder laufende Zahlungen zu erwarten haben, durch eingeschriebenen Brief gemäß Vordruck Dev. VI 5 Nr. 3

zu benachrichtigen, daß Sie Zahlungen nur noch auf Ihrem beschränkt verfügbaren Sicherungskonto entgegennehmen dürfen und daß Barzahlungen an Sie oder Zahlungen zu Ihren Gunsten an dritte Personen nicht mehr
zulässig sind.

2. Die Mitteilungen sind binnen f ü n f T a g e n nach Zustellung der Sicherungsanordnung, soweit
jedoch die Zahlungsverpflichtung erst in Zukunft entstehen sollte, sofort nach ihrer Entstehung a b z u s e n d e n.
Von den einzelnen Mitteilungen haben Sie Zweitschriften zu fertigen und die P o s t e i n l i e f e r u n g s -
s c h e i n e auf diese aufzukleben.

3. Die Zweitschriften dieser Mitteilungen haben Sie mir zusammen mit Vordruck VI Dev. 3 Nr. 2 einzureichen, soweit die Zahlungsverpflichtungen erst in Zukunft entstehen, sofort nach Absendung der einzelnen
Mitteilungen.

IV. Sondervorschriften für Gewerbebetriebe und Grundbesitz.

1. Diese Sicherungsanordnung erstreckt sich nicht auf Vermögenswerte, die dem getrennt verwalteten
Betriebsvermögen eines I h n e n g e h ö r i g e n G e w e r b e b e t r i e b e s zuzurechnen sind. P r i v a t -
e i n n a h m e n dürfen jedoch nicht in bar, sondern n u r d u r c h Ü b e r w e i s u n g auf Ihr beschränkt
verfügbares Sicherungskonto erfolgen.

2. Falls Sie G r u n d s t ü c k s e i g e n t ü m e r sind und einen deutschblütigen Hausverwalter bestellt
haben, gilt folgendes:

  a) M i e t e n darf nur der Hausverwalter von den Mietern entgegennehmen.

  b) Z a h l u n g e n z u I h r e n G u n s t e n a n d r i t t e P e r s o n e n darf der Hausverwalter
  nur insoweit leisten, als sie zur Verwaltung des Grundstücks erforderlich sind.

  c) Der Hausverwalter hat über sämtliche Einnahmen und Ausgaben der Hausverwaltung zwecks jeder-
  zeitiger Prüfung durch die Devisenstelle oder die Zollfahndungsstelle l a u f e n d B u c h z u f ü h r e n.

  d) Sie haben den Hausverwalter gemäß Vordruck Dev. VI 3 Nr. 3 zu benachrichtigen und ihm Kenntnis
  von dieser Sicherungsanordnung zu geben.

V. Sondervorschriften für Ihre Ehefrau und Ihre Kinder.

1. Für den Fall, daß Sie verheiratet sind, minderjährige Kinder haben und I h r e E h e f r a u o d e r
I h r e K i n d e r e i g e n e s V e r m ö g e n b e s i t z e n o d e r i n Z u k u n f t n o c h e r w e r b e n,
ordne ich folgendes an:

  a) Diese Sicherungsanordnung gilt entsprechend auch für Ihre Ehefrau und Ihre minderjährigen Kinder.
  Sie haben Ihre Ehefrau sofort von dieser Sicherungsanordnung in Kenntnis zu setzen.

  b) Ihre Ehefrau und Ihre minderjährigen Kinder dürfen über ihre zu errichtenden beschränkt verfügbaren Sicherungskonten n u r mit schriftlicher Genehmigung der Devisenstelle verfügen; eine Genehmigung ist n i c h t erforderlich zu Überträgen und Überweisungen auf I h r beschränkt verfügbares Sicherungskonto. I h r e r E h e f r a u u n d I h r e n K i n d e r n steht ein be-
  s o n d e r e r m o n a t l i c h e r F r e i b e t r a g in keinem Falle zu.

VI. Nachweisung der vorgenommenen Verfügungen.

Die D e v i s e n b a n k, bei der das beschränkt verfügbare Sicherungskonto geführt wird, h a t e i n e
A u f s t e l l u n g a l l e r V e r f ü g u n g e n ü b e r d i e s e s K o n t o a n z u f e r t i g e n; in der Aufstellung müssen Tag, Betrag und Grund der geleisteten Zahlungen sowie Name und Anschrift der Zahlungs-
empfänger zu ersehen sein. Ich behalte mir vor, diese Aufstellung zwecks Prüfung einzufordern.

VII. Strafvorschrift, Nichtigkeit, Anträge und Anfragen.

1. Zuwiderhandlungen gegen diese Sicherungsanordnung und Umgehungen sind mit h o h e r F r e i - h e i t s - u n d G e l d s t r a f e bedroht (§ 69, Abs. 1 Ziff. 6 des Devisengesetzes).

2. Geschäfte, die gegen die Sicherungsanordnung verstoßen, sind n i c h t i g (§ 64 Abs. 1 des Devisen- gesetzes).

3. A n t r ä g e u n d A n f r a g e n , die sich auf die Sicherungsanordnung beziehen, sind g r u n d - s ä t z l i c h d u r c h V e r m i t t l u n g d e r D e v i s e n b a n k e i n z u r e i c h e n , bei der Ihr beschränkt verfügbares Sicherungskonto geführt wird. Anträge und Anfragen, die unmittelbar bei der Devisenstelle ein- gereicht werden, werden unbearbeitet zurückgegeben.

Jede Änderung Ihrer Anschrift haben Sie mir unverzüglich mitzuteilen.

Im Auftrage

P.S. Die früher gegen Sie erlassenen Sicherungsanordnungen
und bezüglich der Sicherungsanordnungen erteilten
Genehmigungen sind ungültig. Alle Bescheide ersuche
ich postwendend zurückzugeben.

Anlagen:

1 Abschrift dieser Anordnung
1 Vordruck Dev. VI 3 Nr. 2
1 Vordruck Dev. VI 3 Nr. 3

Zur dringenden Beachtung:

Für Anträge auf Freigabe gesicherter Beträge sind grundsätzlich die bei den Devisenbanken oder der Devisenstelle vorrätigen Antragsvordrucke (Vordruck Dev. VI 3 Nr. 5) zu benützen.

Accompanying his letter of April 15, 1940 (Doc. 4), in which he points out that his wife is an American citizen and that her children are entitled to preferential treatment as immigrants in accordance with American immigration laws, Felix Frühauf submitted a list of the goods to be shipped to his wife, Hilde Frühauf (Doc. 5), in a "lift" (a large wooden container) at her New York address. Felix Frühauf also lists several articles of his own as part of the shipment (Doc. 6).

DOCUMENT 4

DOCUMENT 5 AND 6 FOLLOW

UMZUGSGUTVERZEICHNIS

Beförderungsart: Lift

5286

05151 19

Name und genaue Anschrift Kennkartennummer: Amerik. Staatsangehörige
des Answanderers: Johanna gen. Zum Antrag vom: 18. April 1940
Hilde Frühauf, New York, 47 St. Washington Ave., früher Meiningen/Thür.
Strasse der SA 18

Lfd. Nr.	Ab= wohn.	Stück	Gegenstand (genaue Bezeichnung)	Ein= kaufs= preis	Zeit = punkt der Anschaf= fung	Bemerkungen
1	I	1	Tische			
2	"	1	Sofas m. Bezügon			
3	"	5	Sessel " "			
4	"	1	Nähtisch m. Inhalt			
5	"	1	kl. Tischchen			
6	"	2	Fussbänke			
7	"	1	Teewagen			
8	"	1	Gläserschrank			
9	"	1	Vitrine			
10	"	1	Bücherschrank			
11	"	1	Schreibschrank			
12	"	8	Stühle			
13	"	1	Satz Tischchen 3 teilig			
14	"	1	Arbeitstisch			Heirats- gut
15	"	1	Zeitungskasten			
16	"	3	Papierkörbe			
17	"	2	Betten m. Nachtischen			
18	"	10	Auflagen tratzen dazu			
19	"	1	Wäscheschrank			
20	"	1	Frisiertoilette			
21	"	1	Chaiselongue m. Decke			
22	"	2	Stühle u. Hocker			
23	"	1	Wandestell			

Umzuegutverzeichnis der Frau Johanna genannt Hilde Frühauf , New York,
Lift)

05151

52861

Lfd. Nr.	lauf. zchn.	Stück	Gegenstand (genaue Bezeichnung)	Ein- kaufs- preis	Zeit- punkt der Anschaf- fung	Bemerkungen
24	"	2	Metallbetten m. Auflagen			
25	"	1	kl. Schränkchen u. 1 kl. Kommode			
26	"	1	Krankentisch			
27	"	1	Liegestuhl m. Polster			
28	"	1	Wäscheschrank			
29	"	1	Gartengarnitur 5 teilig m. Polster			
30	"	3	Hocker			
31	"	1	Küchentisch, 2 Stühle,			
32	"	1	Flurgarderobe			
33	"	1	Couch umgearbeitet	120.-	1935	2
34	"	2	Plattbretter m.Gestellen, Decken,			
35	"	1	Kleiderbüste			
36	"	40	Deutsche , Lehrbücher u. Gebetbücher			Heirats-
37	"	1	Nähtisch m. Inhalt			gut
38	"	1	Rauchtisch			
39	"	1	Apothekerschränkchen m.Inhalt	5.-	1934	1
40	"	1	Sessel, 2 Stühle u.Hocker			
41	"	2	Stehlampen			
42	"	15	Bilder m. Rahmen			
43	"	1	Album m. 12 Platten			
44	"	1	Kegelspiel			
45	"	1	russ. Teekessel			
46	"	1	Porzellanaufsatz			
47	"	9	Teegläser m. Untersatz			
48	"	4	gr. Tassen m. Teller			
49	"	3	Waschkörbe			
50	"	2	Wäscheleinen u. Klammern			
51	"	2	Waschwannen			
52	"	1	Personenwaage			
53	"	1	Küchenwaage m. Gewichten			
54	"	1	Waffeleisen			
55	"	20	Kochtöpfe			

Umzugsgutverzeichnis Lift) der Frau Joahnna genannt Hilde ....
New York.

Blatt 3)

05151

5280..

lfd. Nr.	Bes. sohe.	Stück	Gegenstand (genaue Bezeichnung)	Firma Monaten preis der Anschaffung	Zeit pacht	Bemerkungen
56	I	1	Eismaschine			
57	I	8	Spülschüsseln			Heiratsgut
58	II	10	Bürsten, wie Spül-,Kleiderbürsten u. Zahrbesen,	8.— 1938		
59	"	4	Gemüseschüsseln u. Bassieren			
60	I	6	Porzellen + u. Em.Schüsseln			
61	"	6	Tontöpfe			
62	"	1	Teppichkehrmaschine			
63	"	8	Zinngefässe			
64	"	1	Bohnerbesen			
65	"	42	Teller u. 7 Platten			
66	"	9	Schüsseln, 3 Pfannen			"
67	"	5	Kuchenformen			
68	"	1	Fliegenschrank			
69		1	Esservice 92 Teile			
70	"	1	Spargelschüssel,			
71	"	12	Obstteller			
72	II	1	Ventilator Nr.8 210 T "Siemens"	10. 15.—	1936 III	
73	I	6	Glasschalen, 5 Glaskrüger			
74	"	5	Blumenvasen			
75	"	2	Kristallaschenbecher			"
76	"	10	Glasuntersetzer			
77	"	12	Gläser			
78	"	1	Porzellanpresse			
79	"	1	Wandspiegel			
80	"	2	Hängelampen			
81	"	1	Inhalierapparat			"
82	"	1	Irrigator			
83	"	5	Kleider-u. Handtuchhalter			
84	"	1	Blumengestell m. 3 Tellerchen			
85	"	16	Sortierleisten u. 24 Gardinenstangen			
86	"	1	Kaffeewärmer			
87	"	2	Eimer			
88	"	1	Satz Schüsseln 5 teilig			

Umzugsgutverzeichnis Lift) der Frau Johanna genannt Hilde Frühauf.
New York, früher Meiningen,   52861

Lfd. Nr.	Abschn	Stück	Gegenstand (genaue Bezeichnung)	Einkauf preis	Zeit-punkt der Anschf.	Bemerkung
89	I	1	Badekorkbrett			
90	"	3	Abtreter			
91	"	1	Klosettrollenhalter m. Papier			
92	"	1	Bohnerbesen			
93	"	1	Toiletteneimer			
94	"	2 P	Skien m. Stöcken			
95	"	idv.	Handwerkzeug, wie Hammer, Beil, Zange Säge etc.			
96	"	1	Urinflasche , 1 Steckbecken			
97	I	2	Tabletts			
98	II	1	Schirm	8.--	1935	
99	I	div.	Schalen, Gelassachen u. Vasen, Gläser			
100	"	"	Decken u. Tücher als Packmaterial			

UMZUGSGUTVERZEICHNIS

Beförderungsart: Lift   als Beipack bei meiner
                         Ehefrau.

05151

52861

Name und genaue Anschrift   Kontokartennummer: J. Meiningen A 00 381
des Auswanderers: Felix Israel   Zum Antrag vom: ......15. JUNI 1940......
rühauf, Meiningen / Thür., Str. der SA 18

Lfd. Nr.	Abs. schn.	Stück	Gegenstand (genaue Bezeichnung)	Einkaufspreis	Zeitpunkt der Anschaffung	Bemerkungen
1	I	1	Schreibmaschine " Ideal B " Nr. 5040			27 Jahre al
2	"	1	Schreibtischlampe			
3	"	3	Abtreter			
4	"	1	Säge , 1 Beil, 1 Gartenschere,			
5	"	div.	Handwerkzeug , wie Hammer, Zange, Meissel etc.			
6	"	1	Zylinderhut m. Kasten			

The contents of the suitcases and hand luggage of the Frühauf children, Helga (Doc. 7) and Rudolf (Doc. 8), and their father (Docs. 9 and 10) also had to be listed down to the last banal detail. The silver knife, fork, and spoon that each was permitted to take as well as some small silver articles (200 grams [7 oz.] per person) and wedding and engagement rings were also listed.

DOCUMENT 7, 8, 9 AND 10 FOLLOW

UMZUGSGUTVERZEICHNIS

Beförderungsart:

Koffer
(Handgepäck)

A 500734
Berlin
18.April 1

Name und genaue Anschrift Helga Sara Trillhaaf Kennkartennummer:
des Auswanderers: Zum Antrag vom: ....
nach New-York 47 Ft.Washington Ave.   Meiningen Strasse der S

Lfd. Nr.	Ab= schn.	Stück	Gegenstand (genaue Bezeichnung)	Ein= kaufs= preis	Zeit= punkt der Anschaf= fung	Bemerkunge
1	11	1	Mantel			
2	II	2	Garnituren	3.-	6- 1938	
3	"	1	Unterrock	3-	1938	s.angefe1
4	"	1	Schlafanzug	6-	1936	"
5	"	1	Korsett	12-	1938	
6	"	6 Pr	Strümpfe	9-	1938	
7		1	Kostüm aus alt.Anzug angefert.			
8	II	2	Sommer Kleider	10.-	18- 1938	s.angefert
9	II	1 Pr	Handschuhe	3-	1938	"
10	II	1	Halstuch	5-	1938	
11	II	3	Hüte aus alten selbst umgearb.			
12	II	1 Pr.	Schuhe 1 Pr Hausschuhe	11-	1937/38	
13	II	2	Taschen m/Inhalt wie Puder,Kamm,Kleidbürse e.c.	12-	"	
14	II	10	Taschentücher	1-		
15	II	2	1 Armband 1 Sportuhr	10.-	1935	Geschenk
16	II	1	Reisenecessaire m/Inhalt	5.-	1935	"
17	III	1	Kulturbeutel "	3-	1937	
18	III	10	Camelia Binden m/Gürtel	1-	1938	
19	III	1	Brillen	12-	1938	
20	II	2	Schirme	6.- 14-	1938/38	
21	I	1	Trinierkragen			
22	I	1	Verlobungsring		1938	
23	II	1	Kästchen m/unech.Schmuck	2.-	1935/38	Geschen
24	II	1	" m/ 2 kleine Karten		1938	"
25	I	div.	engl. Lehrbücher & Hefte			
26	II	1	Koffer		1935	"
27	II	div.	Etui wie Nüh-Bilder-Cigaret.	3.-	1935	"
28	I	1	e ...tift			
29	I		400 g. Silber			
30	I	2	Blusen aus alten Stoff c.angefert.			

Blatt2

Umzugsgutverzeichnis des Felix Israel Frühauf, Meiningen / Thr.
Strasse der SA 18,
|Handgepäck)

Lfd. Nr.	Abschn.	Stück	Gegenstand (genaue Bezeichnung)	Einkaufspreis	Zeitpunkt der Anschf.	Bemerkung
30	I	2	mal 4 teiliges Essbesteck			
31	"	200	g erlaubtes Silber			
32	II	1	Spiel Karten im Etui	1.-	1931	
33	I	1	Fläschchen im Lederetui			
34	"	1	Bund Kofferschlüssel			
35	II	1	Beutel m. Toilettenartikel	2.--	1938	
36	I	2	Koffer u. 2 Schimmhüllen			
37	"	2	Brieftaschen			
38	I	1	Aktenmappe m/Inhalt			

UMZUGSGUTVERZEICHNIS
Beförderungsart: Koffer (Handgepäck)

Name und genaue Anschrift   A oo164 Meiningen
des Auswanderers: Kennkartennummer: 18.April 1940.
nach New-York   Zum Antrag vom:

Lfd. Nr.	Ab= schn.	Stück	Gegenstand (genaue Bezeichnung)	Ein= kaufs= preis	Zeit= punkt der Anschfg.	Bemerkungen.
1	II		Oberhemden	8.--	1937	
2	II	2 P	Strümpfe	4.- 7.5c	1938	
3	I	1	Schaal 1 Pr.Handschuhe			
4	II	2	Kravatten	3.--	1938	
5	"	1	Garnitur	2.5c	1937	s.angefert
6	II	je 1	Nachthemd und	4.--	1936/37	"
7	I	1	Pullover v.Vater			
8	II		Taschentücher	3.--	1935	
9	II	je 1	Hut und eine Mütze	3.- 8.5c	1936	
1o	I	je 1	Regenmantel v.Onkel,Anzug v.Vater geändert			
11	I	" 1	P. Hausschuhe Schuhe v.Vater		1935	
12	II	1	Reisenecessaire m/Inhalt		1935	Geschenk
13	II	1	Toilettenbeutel m/Inhalt m/Inhalt		1935	"
14	I	1	Rasier-Ap. mit Klingen			
15	I	1	Armband-Uhr			
16	II	1	" "	15.-	1935	" Zinse
17	II	1	Brieftasche Geldbörse		1935	" "
18	II	je1	Füllfeder Bleistat.i.Etui	3.-	1935	" "
19	II	" 1	Cigaret.Etui Federmessd	1.-	1935	" "
2o	I	1	Stock			
21	I	div.T.	Messer, Feilbuch, Gürtel 1 Sonnenbrille, 1 Pfeife			
22	II	1	Wecker	2.-	1936	" "
23	I	1 K	6 teiliges Essbesteck			
24	I	2oo g.	Silber			
25	I	1	Schirm			
26	I	1	Koffer			

Umzugsgutverzeichnis

Beförderungsart: Koffer (Reisegepäck)

Name und genaue Anschrift des Auswanderers:
Felix Israel Wilhauf
Meiningen / Thüringen, Str. der SA 18

Kennkartennummer : J.Meininge
Zum Antrag vom: 15.JUNI 1940

Lfd. Nr.	Ab-schn	Stück	Gegenstand (genaue Bezeichnung)	Einkaufspreis	Zeitpunkt der Ansch.	Bemerkungen
1	I	je	1 Auszeichnung , wie K.E. II, u. Ehrenkreuz f. Frontkämpfer			
2	"	1	Frack u. 1 Smoking			
3	"	1	schwarzen Anzug			
4	"	2	Arbeitsanzüge			
5	II	2	Winteranzüge, Stoffe v. 1933			
6	I	je	1 Haus - u. 1 Sommerjoppe			
7	II	1	Wintermantel	80.- 60.-	1937	
8	I	1	Übergangs -u. 1 Staubmantel			
9	II	2	Hüte	10.- 15.-	1937/38	
10	I	10 2	Oberhemden			
11	II	5 2	" "	15.-	1936	Geburtstagsgeschenk
12	III	3	Kravatten	9.-	1939	
13	I	8 2	Kravatten u. Schleifen			
14	II	4	"		1936	"
15	I	2	Schals			
16	I	1	Unterziehweste			
17	"	6	Nachthemden			
18	II	5	"	9.-		"
19	I	2 Dtz.	Taschentücher	3.-		
20	II	12	"	3.-		"
21	I	14 P.	Strümpfe			

Blatt 2

Umzugsgutverzeichnis des Felix Israel Frühauf, Meiningen / Thür.
Nr. der SA 18

Lfd. Nr.	Abschn.	Stück	Gegenstand (genaue Bezeichnung)	Ein-kaufs-preis	Zeit-punkt der Anschf.	Bemerkung
22	I	10	Wintergarnituren (Unterwäsche)			
23	II	6	Sommergarnituren "	9.—	1936	Geb.Gesch
24	"	6 P	Strümpfe	9.—	"	" "
25	I	2	Kästen m. 35 Kragen			
26	"	5 "	Handschuhe			
27	"	1 P	Lackschuhe u. 1 P. Sommerschuhe			
28	II	2 "	Schuhe	25.—	1936/38	
29	I	2 "	Hausschuhe u. 1 P.Filzpantoffel			
30	"	1 "	Gummischuhe			
31	"	1	Rasierapparat m. Zubehör			
32	"	div.	Bürsten u. Kämme			
33	"	2	Schirme u.(3 Stöcke)			
34	"	2 P	Gamaschen			
35	II je	1 "	Strumpfhalter u. Hosenträger	3.—	1938	
36	"	1	Kasten m. Knöpfen, Senkel, Er-satzteilen, Einlegsohlen, Schuhanzieher	4.—	1938	
37	"	1	Gebetmantel, 1 P. Gebetriemen,			
38	I	1	Aktentasche m. Inhalt			
39	"	1	Schreibmappe, 1 Lineal, 1 Locher, 1 Brieföffner,2 Füllfederhalter			
40	"	1	Kasette u. 1 Kästchen m. Würfel			
41	"	1	Namenschild			
42	"	div.	Kleiderbügel u. Kleiderhüllen			
43	"	5	Koffer			

UMZUGSGUTVERZEICHNIS

Beförderungsart: Koffer (Handgepäck)

Peter Frühauf

| J.Meiningen A 00 381 |

Name und genaue Anschrift   Kennkartennummer:
Peter Frühauf Mainauf, Meiningen/ Thür. .... 15. JUNI 1940 ....

Lfd. Nr.	Ab- schn.	Stück	Gegenstand (genaue Bezeichnung)	Ein- kaufs- preis	Zeitpunkt der Anschaf- fung	Bemerkungen
1	II	1	Hut u. 1 Mütze	12.--	1937	
2	I	2	Anzüge			
3	II	1	Anzug	40.-- 65.--	1938	
4	I	1	Regenmantel			
5	"	3	Oberhemden			
6	II	2	"	10.--	1936	Geburt.Gesch
7	"	3	Garnituren		"	" "
8	"	2 P	Schuhe	25.--	1937/38	
9	I	1 "	Hausschuhe im Etui			
10	II	9 "	Strümpfe		1936	" "
11	II	1 "	Hosenträger u. 1 P.Sockenhalter		"	" "
12	I	2	Nachthemden m. Hülle			
13	II	1	Rasierapparat m. Zubehör	7,50	1938	
14	II	1	Reiseetui m. Inhalt		1936	" "
15	III	1	Flasche Kopfwasser u. Rasierwasser	3,50	1939	
16	I	1 P	Handschuhe u. 6 Taschentücher			
17	II	2	Kravatten	4.- 7.--	1938	
18	I	5	Kragen, 1 Handtuch			
19	II	3	Brillen	3.-		
20	II	1	Nickelarmbanduhr als Ersatz für eine abgegebene goldene Uhr			
21	""	1	Füllfederhalter	5,85	1938	
22	I	3	Drehstifte, 2 Messer,1 Wecker			
23	"	1	Geldbörse, 1 Brieftasche m. Inhalt			
24	"	1	Feuerzeug , 1 Zigarrenetui			
25	III	div.	Zigarren	5.--	1939	
26	I	1	Trauring, 1 Notizbuch			
27	"	1	Rehdecke m. Riemen			
28	"	1	Manikure			
29	"	2	Sportgürtel			

On September 19, 1940, a senior bailiff named Bechmann of the court in Hildburghausen drew up an inventory of the items Hilde Frühauf (Doc. 11) and her husband, Felix Frühauf (Doc. 13), respectively, planned to take with them (in hand luggage and suitcases) and which were acquired after December 31, 1932. Each item, however small and insignificant, was checked and its assessed value entered on the list. This degrading process was preceded by the issuance by the local municipal authority of a document certifying that the Frühaufs owed no outstanding taxes. The costs connected with the preparation of these inventories were also billed to and paid by the Frühaufs (Docs. 12 and 14).

DOCUMENT 11 FOLLOWS

```
                    - Von Sachverständigen ausfüllen -
                                                                    Blatt 1
Otto Bechmann , Obergerichtsvollzieher
                  in Hildburghausen            Meiningen,den 19.Sept.1940
als Vetreter des Oberger.Vlz.Höhn in
              Meiningen
                         T a x - V e r z e i c h n i s
  DR.1197  der zur Mitnahme ins Ausland bestimmten Umzugsgüter
    /40   die nach dem 31.12.1932 angeschafft worden sind.
              Gesch.-Z.der Devisenstelle: II J Tr/L.  10145/5
              Name des Auswanderes:Johanna gen. Hilde Frühauf geb. Schwerin
              Anschrift:  New-York  USA. 47 Ft. Washington Ave.
```

Gegenstand (genaue Bezeichnung)	Jahr der Anschaffung	Einkaufs-Preis lt.	Taxwert d. Sachverst.	Bemerkung
Medikamente,Scheren,Schalen u. Verbandsstoff	1938/39	25.--	25.--	Reisegepäck
Gummiwarmflasche	1935	2.--	2.--	
Kasten m.Toilettenseife	1938	2.--	2.--	
2 Winterschlüpfer	1937	7.--	7.--	
12 Garnituren m.Brettchen	1936/38	42.--	42.--	
2 Schlafanzüge	1938	6.50	6.50	
8 Nachthemden	1938	24.--	12.--	
2 1/2 Dtz.Strümpfe	1936/38	55.--	30.--	
6 Kittelschürzen	1937/38	30.--	10.--	
2 Flaschen Parfüm	1938/39	4.--	4.--	
2 Schirme	1938	25.--	25.--	
2 Handtaschen	1938/39	23.--	23.--	
20 Camelia	1939	1.--	1.--	
1 Wintermantel	1936	70.--	70.--	
2 Sommermäntel	1938	70.--	70.--	
1 Übergangsmantel	1937	50.--	40.--	
4 Winterkleider	1935/36	60.--	60.--	
7 Sommerkleider	1935/38	90.--	60.--	
2 Röcke	1936/38	20.--	20.--	
1 Bluse 1	1938	12.--	12.--	
5P.Schuhe m.Spanner,Hüllen	1935/38	50.--	30.--	
1 Schreibmaschine	1935	160.--	70.--	
Kasten m.Waschmittel	1932/37	12.--	12.--	
2 Puderdosen	1937	3.--	3.--	
1 Drehbleistift	1938	3.--	3.--	
Schneiderartikel,Scheren	1936/37	60.--	60.--	
Backgeräte	1938	5.--	5.--	
Glaskochgeräte	1937/38	12.--	12.--	
2 Mops	1936/38	5.--	5.--	
2 Spülschüsseln	1936/38	5.--	5.--	
1 Staubzauger	1933	150.--	50.--	
Bürsten und Besen	1936/38	12.--	12.--	
Schrubber und Bürsten	1936/38	2.--	2.--	
Schuhputz	1938	2.--	2.--	
1 Wachstuch	1939	3.50	3.50	
1 Waffeleisen	1938	10.--	8.--	
12 Büchsen m.Heiltee	1939	5.--	5.--	
1 Bettsack	1936	20.--	10.--	
3 Koffer	1935/38	35.--	35.--	
1 Brille	1939	8.--	8.--	
1 Reisewecker	1938	12.--	10.--	
1 Fahrband	1939	2.--	2.--	
Schreibpapier mit Quwerts	1939	3.--	3.--	

```
                      Übertrag Blatt 2       M  877.--
```

Gegenstand (genaue Bezeichnung)	Jahr der Anschaffung.	Einkaufspreis.	Taxwert d.Sachverständigen	Blatt 2 Bemerkung
Übertrag von Blatt 1			877.--	05151
1 Wintermantel	1937	35.--	10.--	Reisegepäck der
2 Pullover	1934/38	6.--	3.--	Tochter Helga
1 Winterkleid	1937	9.--	2.--	Sara Frühauf
6 Sommerkleider	1935/3	6.--	30.--	
1 Kapuze	1939	2.--	2.--	
4 Büstenhalter	1936/38	6.--	6.--	52861
1 Dtz. Winterstrümpfe	1937/38	18.--	18.--	
6P. Schuhe	1936/38	48.--	30.--	
3 Handtaschen	1935/36	15.--	5.--	
3 Hutformen	1938	6.--	2.--	
Schreibutensilien	1935/37	6.--	6.--	
Toilettenartikel	1938	15.--	15.--	
Toilettenartikel	1939	15.--	15.--	
Camelia	1939	1.--	1.--	
8 Garnituren I	1938	32.--	24.--	Reisegepäck des
8 Oberhemden	1935/38	28.--	12.--	Sohnes Rudolf
10 Krawatten	1937/38	15.--	5.--	Israel Frühauf
12 Taschentücher	1938	6.--	2.--	
2 Arbeitsanzüge	1937/38	70.--	30.--	
2 Hosen	1938	30.--	10.--	
2P Schuhe	1937/38	20.--	8.--	
Stiefelknecht	1939	--.40	--.40	
1 Rasierapparat	1935		2.--	
1 Schreibmappe	1936		2.--	
2 Garnituren	1938	6.--	3.--	Handgepäck Toch
2 Sommerkleider	1938	14.--	10.--	
2 Taschen m. Inhalt	1937/38	12.--	12.--	
1 Armband,18portuhr	1935		10.--	
1Reisenessesär	1935		5.--	
1 Kulturbeutel	1937	7.--	5.--	
2 Brillen	1939	17.--	12.--	
3 Schirme	1935/38	14.--	6.--	
1 Kästchen m. unechtschmuck	1936/38		2.--	
1 Etui m.Inhalt	1935		2.--	
5P Strümpfe	1938	7.50	4.--	Klingepäck Sohn
1 Hut u.Mütze	1938	8.50	3.--	
1 Toilettenbeutel m.Inhalt	1935	6.--	6.--	
1 Armbanduhr	1935		15.--	
Füllfederhalter u.Bleist.	1935		3.--	
Zigarettenetui u.Anzünder	1935		1.--	
1 Wecker	1935		2.--	
1 Couch	1935	120.--	60.--	Lift Johanna Frü
Inhalt von Apothekenschrank	1939		5.--	auf
Bürsten u.Besen	1938	8.--	8.--	
Ventilator	1936	15.--	10.--	
1 Schirm I	1935	8.--	8.--	

M 1 3 1 0.40

Anerkannt für Johanna gen.Hilde Frühauf
und als ges.Vertreter meiner Kinder

Kennkarte: Meiningen Nr. A00 381

Nachrichtlich:

Obergerichtsvollzieher.

DOCUMENT 12

Kostenrechnung

Für die Prüfung und Schätzung des Umzugsgutes
der Johanna gen. Hilde Frühauf, New-York 47 Ft. Washington Ave
Sachgebiet: II J Tr/L.   Gesch.Nr. 10145/5
DR: Nr. 1197/40

RM   26.20   Gebühren § 2 der Gebühren Ordnung für die Prüfung von
             Umzugsgut durch den Gerichtsvollzieher als Sachverständi-
             ger der Devisenstelle
RM   2.80   Fahrgeld
RM   -.50   Schreibgebühr
RM   -.24   Porto
RM   -.05   Vordrucke
RM   29.79

Diesen Betrag zahlte heute der Antragsteller in bar.
Quittung ist erteilt.
Die Kosten werden in dem Register des Gerichtsvollziehers Franke in Mei-
ningen unter der Nr. 1197/40 erfasst.

                                        Meiningen, den 19. Sept. 1940
Dienstsiegel   gez. Bechmann
                                        Obergerichtsvollzieher

DOCUMENT 13

— Vom Sachverständigen auszufüllen —

Blatt 1

Otto Bechmann , Obergerichtsvollzieher Meiningen, den 19. September 1940
Name des Sachverständigen in Hildburghausen Ort, Datum

als Vetreter des Oberger.Vlz. Höhn in Meiningen

DR 1193/40

Tax=Verzeichnis

05151

der zur Mitnahme ins Ausland bestimmten Umzugsgüter,
die nach dem 31.12.1932 angeschafft worden sind.

Gesch.-Z. der Devisenstelle: II 3 Tr/L. 10145/6

Name des Auswanderers: Felix Israel Frühauf

Anschrift: Meiningen/Thüringen Strasse der SA 18

Gegenstand (genaue Bezeichnung)	Jahr der Anschaffung	Einkaufspreis lt. Rechnung	Taxwert des Sachverständigen	Bemerkungen
Hut u.Mütze	1937	12.--	12.--	Handgepäck
1 Anzug	1938	65.--	40.--	
2 Oberhemden	1936		10.--	
1 Rasierappar	1938	7.50	7.50	
Kopf-u.Rasier- wasser	1939	3.50	3.50	
2 Krawatten	1938	7.--	4.--	
3 Brillen			3.--	
1 Füllhalter	1938	5.85	5.85	
Zigarren	1939	5.--	5.--	
Spielkarten	1939		1.--	
Toilettenart.	1938	2.--	2.--	
Wintermantel	1937	60.--	30.--	Reisegepäck
2 Hüte	1937/38	15.--	10.--	
5 Oberhemden	1936		15.--	
3 Krawatten	1939	9.--	9.--	
3 Nachthemden	1936		9.--	
12 Taschentüch.	36		3.--	
6 Sommergarnit.	36		9.--	
6P.Strümpfe	1936		9.--	
2P. Schuhe	1936/38	25.--	20.--	
Strumpfhalter u.Hosenträger	1938	3.--	3.--	
			210.85	

Gegen diese Schätzung steht dem Antragsteller der sofortige kostenpflichtige Einspruch zu. Der Einspruch
ist dadurch zu erheben, daß der Antragsteller seiner Unterschrift die Worte: „Ich erhebe Einspruch" hinzufügt
und das Wort „Anerkannt" streicht.

Falls der Raum oben nicht ausreicht, ist die Rückseite oder ein Zusatz zu benützen.

K 318

DOCUMENT 14

Kostenrechnung

für die Prüfung und Schätzung des Umzugsgutes
des Felix Israel Frühauf, Meiningen / Thür. Strasse der SA 18
Sachgebiet: II J Tr. / L.   Gesch.-Nr. 10145 / 6
DR. Nr. 1193 / 40

RM 20.–   Gebühren § 2 der Gebühren Ordnung für die Prüfung von
           Umzugsgut durch den Gerichtsvollzieher als Sachverständi-
           ger der Devisenstelle
RM –.50   Schreibgebühr
RM –.05   Vordrucke
RM 20.55

Diesen Betrag zahlte heute der Antragsteller in bar.
Quittung ist erteilt.
Die Kosten werden in dem Register des Gerichtsvollziehers Franke in Mei-
ningen unter der Nr. 1193 / 40 erfasst.

Dienstsiegel   Meiningen, den 19. September 1940
                                      gez. Bechmann
                                      Obergerichtsvollzieher

On September 24, 1940, the Foreign Currency Office of the Regional Office of the Finance Ministry in Rudolstadt ordered Felix Frühauf to pay a nonrefundable fee of 400 marks to the Deutsche Golddiskontbank (German Gold Discount Bank) in Berlin. In addition, the letter stipulated that he either sell privately the things he was not permitted to take abroad or deliver them to the clothing collection center in Erfurt (Doc. 15).

After an appeal, Felix Frühauf was permitted to hand over three shirts instead of five, eight pair of socks instead of twelve. His son, Rudolf, was allowed to hand over three pair of socks instead of five, and his daughter, Helga, five handkerchiefs instead of seven. They had to present the various receipts (e.g., Docs. 16 and 17) showing that they had disposed of the items they were not allowed to take with them.

On November 21, Felix Frühauf submitted a document from the Sparkasse (savings bank) confirming the fact that the 400 marks had been paid [doc. not reproduced here].

DOCUMENT 15

Der Oberfinanzpräsident Thüringen
(Devisenstelle)

Rudolstadt,
24. September 1940
Schwarzburger Straße 60
Fernsprecher 5 22 und 5 25
Sprechzeit: nur 9–12 Uhr

Herrn
Felix Israel Frühauf

Meiningen
Strasse der SA 18

Dev. / II J 10145 / 6. Tr.L.
(Bitte in jeder Zuschrift angeben)

Betr. Mitnahme von Umzugsgut nach dem Ausland.

Sie erhalten anbei die Aufforderung zur Zahlung einer ersatzlosen Abgabe an die Deutsche Golddiskontbank, Berlin, in Höhe von RM 400.–. Des weiteren ordne ich an, dass Sie die in beigefügten Aufstellungen aufgeführten Gegenstände, deren Mitnahme in das Ausland nicht zulässig ist, entweder freihändig veräussern oder an die zuständige Bezirks- oder Zweigstelle der Reichsvereinigung der Juden in Deutschland, Abteilung Fürsorge – Kleiderkammer, abliefern. Für den hiesigen Bezirk ist die »Kleiderkammer der Bezirksfürsorgestelle Erfurt der Reichsvereinigung der Juden in Deutschland« zuständig. Die Genehmigung zur Mitnahme des Umzugsgutes kann erst dann erteilt werden, wenn mir

1. der Nachweis über die Zahlung der ersatzlosen Abgabe an die Deutsche Golddiskontbank erbracht und
2. die Veräusserung oder die Ablieferung der Gegenstände an die Kleiderkammer nachgewiesen worden ist.

Sobald dieser Nachweis hier vorliegt, werde ich Ihnen die beantragte Genehmigung einsenden.

Im Auftrage

Anlagen.   gez. Unterschrift

DOCUMENT 16

Ich habe heute von Herrn Felix Israel Frühauf

1 Pr. Herrnschuhe	für	RMk. 8,–
von Fräulein Helga Sara Frühauf		
1 Pr. Damenschuhe		3,–
1 Reiseplätteisen		4,–

gekauft.   RMk. 15,–
Den Betrag habe ich auf Postscheck-Konto 2534 überwiesen.

Meiningen, den 29. Oktober 1940.   Kurt Reichenbacher
                                                                                    Meiningen

DOCUMENT 17

Ich habe heute von meiner Gross-Kusine Helga Sara Frühauf in Meiningen geschenkt erhalten:

1 Regenmantel
5 Pr. Strümpfe
1 Sommer- 1 Winterkleid
1 Pullover
1 Bluse
3 Schürzen
6 Waschlappen
3 Taschentücher

Meiningen, den 27. Oktober 1940.

gez. Ellen Rei:
Poppenlauer

Notice from the Main Customs Office in Meiningen listing the charges and fees owed for the last of three days of preparation and packing of the goods to be shipped abroad. Two officials closed and sealed the lift (a wooden container used to move personal goods) on January 9, 1941, for which they were paid a fee (Doc. 18). The officials as well as Felix Frühauf signed written declarations asserting that no currency, stocks or bonds, gold or other precious metals, or other such valuables had been packed in the lift (Doc. 19). In addition, since it was wintertime, Felix Frühauf and his children were given written permission to take specific necessary items of clothing such as coats, hats, and so forth along in their hand luggage (Doc. 20).

DOCUMENT 18

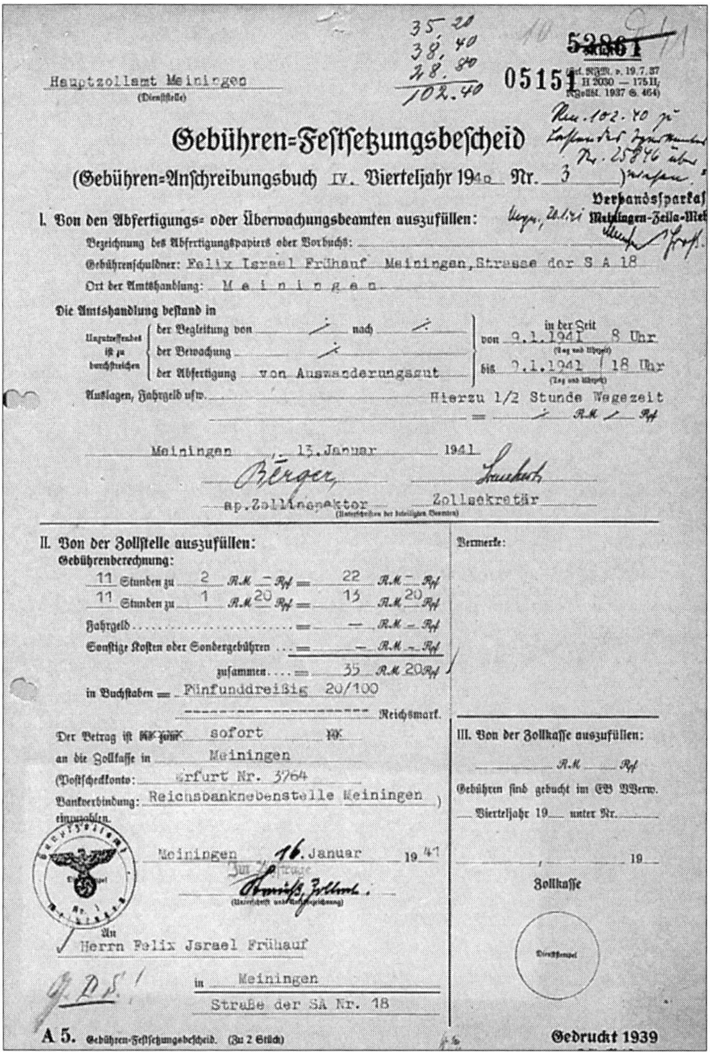

Hauptzollamt Meiningen
(Dienststelle)

35.20
38.40
28.80
102.40

05151

(Vgl. RdF. v. 19.7.37 H 2030 — 175 II; RZollBl. 1937 S. 464)

Gebühren=Festsetzungsbescheid

(Gebühren=Anschreibungsbuch IV. Vierteljahr 1940 Nr. 3)

Verbandssparkasse Meiningen-Zella-Mehlis

I. Von den Abfertigungs= oder Überwachungsbeamten auszufüllen:

Bezeichnung des Abfertigungspapiers oder Vorbuchs:

Gebührenschuldner: Felix Israel Frühauf Meiningen, Strasse der S A 18

Ort der Amtshandlung: M e i n i n g e n

Die Amtshandlung bestand in

(Unzutreffendes ist zu durchstreichen)
- der Begleitung von – nach –
- der Bewachung –
- der Abfertigung von Auswanderungsgut

in der Zeit von 9.1.1941 8 Uhr (Tag und Uhrzeit) bis 9.1.1941 18 Uhr (Tag und Uhrzeit)

Auslagen, Fahrgeld usw. Hierzu 1/2 Stunde Wegezeit = – RM – Rpf

Meiningen, 13. Januar 1941

Berger — Zollsekretär
ap. Zollinspektor
(Unterschriften der beteiligten Beamten)

II. Von der Zollstelle auszufüllen:

Gebührenberechnung:

11 Stunden zu	2 RM	– Rpf	=	22 RM	– Rpf
11 Stunden zu	1 RM	20 Rpf	=	13 RM	20 Rpf
Fahrgeld			=	– RM	– Rpf
Sonstige Kosten oder Sondergebühren			=	– RM	– Rpf
zusammen			=	35 RM	20 Rpf

in Buchstaben = Fünfunddreißig 20/100 Reichsmark.

Vermerke:

Der Betrag ist sofort an die Zollkasse in Meiningen (Postscheckkonto: Erfurt Nr. 3764 Bankverbindung: Reichsbanknebenstelle Meiningen) einzuzahlen.

Meiningen, 16. Januar 1941
Im Auftrage
(Unterschrift und Amtsbezeichnung)

An Herrn Felix Jsrael Frühauf in Meiningen Straße der SA Nr. 18

III. Von der Zollkasse auszufüllen:

RM Rpf

Gebühren sind gebucht im EB VVerw.

Vierteljahr 19 unter Nr.

, 19

Zollkasse

Dienststempel

A 5. Gebühren-Festsetzungsbescheid. (Zu 2 Stück) Gedruckt 1939

DOCUMENT 19

Erklärung

Ich erkläre hiermit, daß sich in dem zur Nachschau vorgeführten Reisegut, nämlich:

ein Lift[1]

Zahlungsmittel, Wertpapiere, Gold, andere Edelmetalle, Bruchmaterial aus Gold oder anderen Edelmetallen, Waren aus Gold oder anderen Edelmetallen, die üblicherweise nicht aus diesen Metallen hergestellt werden, oder Handelswaren nicht befinden.

gez.: Meiningen, 11. Januar 1941
Felix Israel Frühauf
Strasse der SA 18
Kennkarte J
Meiningen A 00381

Abfertigungsbefund

Bei der Nachschau wurden weder Zahlungsmittel, Wertpapiere, Gold und Edelmetalle, noch sonstige ausfuhrverbotene oder ausfuhrzollpflichtige Waren vorgefunden.

Der Lift ist mit vier Zollplomben T 84 verschlossen worden.

Meiningen, 11. Januar 1941
Dienstsiegel   gez. Unterschriften

1 Damals gebräuchliches Wort für Umzugscontainer.

DOCUMENT 20

Bescheinigung

Meiningen, den 11. Januar 1941.

Dem Herrn Felix Frühauf in Meiningen, Strasse der SA 18, wird hiermit bescheinigt, dass die mit Bescheid des Herrn Oberfinanzpräsidenten Thüringen (Devisenstelle) vom 23. Nov. 1940 – Dev. II J 10145/6 Tr./L. nachstehend zur Ausfuhr genehmigten Gegenstände im Reisegepäck nicht mit verpackt worden sind.
Diese Gegenstände können im Handgepäck mitgeführt werden.

1. einen Wintermantel
2. ein Paar Gummischuhe
3. einen Gebet-Mantel u. Riemen
4. eine Mütze und ein Muff
5. einen Regenmantel
6. zwei Schlüpfer
7. eine Wolljacke
8. eine Bettjacke
9. zwei Schürzen
10. ein Paar Überschuhe
11. ein Nähetui m/Inhalt
12. ein Skianzug m/Zubehör
13. einen Gebetmantel u. Riemen
14. ein Paar Hosenträger
15. ein Sommermantel
16. ein Wintermantel
17. eine Reisedecke
18. eine kleine elektr. Lampe

Dienstsiegel   gez. Unterschriften

Certificate of Good Conduct issued to the twenty-one-year-old
Helga Sara Frühauf, dated February 7, 1941 (Doc. 21), and an extension dated June 6, 1941 (Doc. 22).

DOCUMENT 21 IS OPPOSITE
DOCUMENT 22 FOLLOWS

Führungszeugnis

De r Helga Sara Frühauf, Meiningen, Str.d.SA 18,

geboren am 19 ten Dez.1920 zu Meiningen, Kr.Meiningen,

wird

bescheinigt, daß er/sie

vom Tage der Geburt bis 12.10.1936

15.4.1939 heute

hier gemeldet und in den polizeilichen Listen als bestraft nicht verzeichnet ist.

Jedes Führungszeugnis hat die Erklärung zu enthalten, daß etwaige Verurteilungen, über die nach dem Reichsgesetz vom 9. April 1920 (Reichsgesetzbl. S. 507) keine Auskunft erteilt werden darf, als nicht verzeichnet behandelt werden.

Meiningen, den 7.2. 19 41
(Ort) (Datum)

Der Bürgermeister

Rev.Oberleutn.d.Schutzpol./B
Unterschrift

Stadtkasse Meiningen
Gebühr 1.00 RM. 41
04073

1.- RM. Gebühr

Thüringer Formularverlag R. Burkmann, Weimar

Das Führungszeugnis Helga Sara Frühauf wird bis 6. 6. 1941
verlängert.

   Strafen sind in den polizeilichen Listen in der Zeit vom
7. 2. 1941 bis heute nicht verzeichnet.

   Geb: 0,50 RM.

Der Bürgermeister
Einw.-Meldeamt
J.A.

Character reference for Helga Frühauf made out by her teacher Theodora Bayer, dated February 21, 1941 (Doc. 23), and character reference for her father, Felix Frühauf, dated March 15, 1941 (Doc. 24). These documents had to be notarized for a fee.

DOCUMENT 23

Leumundszeugnis

Helga Frühauf geb. am 19. Dez. 1920 zu Meiningen Tochter des Kaufmanns Felix Frühauf und dessen verstorbenen Ehefrau Frau Hilde geb. Schwerin ist der Unterzeichneten seit dem Jahre 1927 bestens bekannt. Die Grundlinien in ihrer Erziehung im Elternhaus wie: Gehorsam, Schaffensfreude, Pflichttreue sind der jugendlichen Seele zu Fleisch und Blut geworden und zugleich Rüstzeug genug zu ihrem bereits heute beträchtlichem hausfraulichem Können. Helga Frühauf ist ein sittlich hochstehendes Menschenkind.

Meiningen, den 21. Februar 1941.
gez. Theodora Bayer
Oberlehrerin

Nr. 56 der Urkundenrolle für 1941.
Die vorstehende eigenhändige Namensunterschrift
des Fräulein Theodora Bayer, Oberlehrerin, wohnhaft in Meiningen,
beglaubige ich hiermit.

Meiningen, den 21. Februar 1941. gez. Unterschrift
Notar.

Kostenberechnung:
2. – RM Gebühr §§ 26, 39 RKO

gez. Unterschrift
Notar.
Dienstsiegel

DOCUMENT 24

Leumundszeugnis

Ich der Unterzeichnete bestätige hiermit, dass Herr Felix Frühauf seit 1901 in Meiningen wohnhaft ist, und mir als ein sehr seriöser, umsichtiger, charaktervoller Kaufmann bekannt, der es durch seine 25jährige Selbständigkeit in der Lederbranche zu einer sehr angesehenen und bekannten Firma gebracht hat.
Herr Frühauf führt ein sehr schönes Familienleben und ist durch sein vornehmes Auftreten sehr beliebt.
Politisch ist Herr Frühauf niemals hervor getreten, und bei keiner Partei betätigt.

Meiningen, den 15. März 1941
gez. Daniel Israel Elsbach

Nr. 94 der Urkundensteuer für 1941.
Die vorstehende eigenhändige Namensunterschrift des mir persönlich bekannten Herrn Daniel Israel Elsbach, wohnhaft in Meiningen, beglaubige ich hiermit.

Meiningen, den 15. März 1941.   gez. Unterschrift
                                                 Notar.

Kostenberechnung:
2.– RM Gebühr §§ 26,39 RKO

gez. Unterschrift
Notar.
Dienstsiegel

The American Express office in Berlin informed Felix Frühauf on February 15, 1941, that his family's passages from Lisbon to New York in the amount of $1,110 had been paid (Doc. 25). Arthur Vomberg, Felix's cousin in the United States, had carried out the transaction.

DOCUMENT 25

Felix Frühauf   Berlin-Charlottenburg, den 26. März 1941
                                        Augsburgerstrasse 37
                                        Pension Werres

An das | Einschreiben-
Amerikanische Generalkonsulat | Einlieferungsschein
Berlin W.9 | vom 26.3.1941
Hermann Göringstrasse 23

Betrifft: Wartenummer 47 591, a,c.

Sehr geehrte Herren!
Zu Ihrer Aufforderung vom 20. ds. Mts. einen Antrag zur Einreise nach USA auf Form 633 zu stellen, erlaube ich mir folgendes schriftlich zu bemerken: Am 25. Februar 1941 wurde ich benachrichtigt, dass meine Beweismittel verjährt seien. Ich habe am 27. November 1940 und 13. Januar 1941 vier Affidavits eingereicht, sowie eine Depotbescheinigung vom 6. Dezember 1940 über $3.000,– Diese Papiere scheinen sich nicht unter meiner Wartenummer 47 591 zu befinden, während Sie in Ihrem Schreiben vom 20. März 1941 eine Nr. 60 119 angeben, die mir unbekannt ist. Ich habe bereits auf Ihre Benachrichtigung vom 10. Januar 1941 eine Buchungsbescheinigung eingereicht und zwar über Fernost, nachdem diese Reise nicht mehr möglich ist habe ich bereits über Lissabon gebucht. Das Passagegeld von $1.650,– ist bereits bei der Export Lines in New York eingezahlt. Die Export Lines wartet auf eine Visaerteilung, um die Schiffskarten uns auszuhändigen.
Ich bitte Sie höflichst wie dringend mir baldmöglichst eine Nachricht zukommen zu lassen.

In vorzüglicher Hochachtung

Felix Frühauf's registered letter of March 26, 1941, to the American Consulate in Berlin (Doc. 26) shows the confusion that reigned there in the matter of his emigration. On January 10 he had already submitted written confirmation that passage had been booked after $1,650 for the ship tickets had been paid to American Export Lines in New York. The latter, however, were asking for proof that he had received the visas before they would make out and send him the tickets.

DOCUMENT 26

American Export Lines in Lisbon sent a letter, dated April 2, 1941, to Feliz [*sic*] Frühauf c/o American Consul in Berlin to the effect that their New York office had informed them that the sum of $1,110 had been paid for ship passages from Lisbon to New York for himself, his daughter Helga, and his son Rudolf, and that accommodations had been reserved on board the *Exeter*, scheduled to sail August 8, 1941 (Doc. 27). These reservations would be canceled if written acceptance did not reach their office in Lisbon by April 27, 1941. The letter mentioned that the matter was also being communicated to the local police and the American Consul in Berlin.

DOCUMENT 27

AMERICAN EXPORT LINES, INC.

25, Broadway, New York, U. S. A.

EXPRESS PASSENGER MAIL AND CARGO STEAMERS
BETWEEN NEW YORK AND LISBON
FAST DIRECT SERVICE

———•■•———

AGENT

JOH. BECKMANN

LISBON.

—

P. O. BOX. N.° 164
TELEGRAPHIC ADDRESS:
"EXPOSHIP"

CODES USED:
Lombard
Bee, old and new edition
ntley's
Scott's 10th edition
TELEPHONES:
2 0394
2 0395
2 0396
2 0397

—

RUA AUREA, 191-1.° & 2.°
LISBON.

—

LISBON, April 2nd 1941

Mr. Feliz Fruehauf
c/o American Consul Berlin

OUR REFERENCE: P.3495

Our New York Office has collected the sum of
$1110,- as already communicated to you

towards passage Lisbon / New York (and taxes) for
yourself, son and daughter

Passage is subject to: a) your possessing valid American
Visa(es); and b) the conditions of the prepaid passage contract
entered into by the purchaser and our American Office. We have
made the following reservation:

Steamer "EXETER"   Scheduled sailing August 8th. 1941

Accommodation guaranteed   Rate —

This reservation will be definitely cancelled unless your
written acceptance is received at this office by 27/4/41

The foregoing is being communicated to the local Police
Authorities and the American Consul at Berlin

Yours very truly,
American Export Lines, Inc.,

F. H. Citriolo.
Mgr. Pass. Dept.

PBC/RLL.

N. B. — ALWAYS MENTION OUR REFERENCE NUMBER WHEN COMMUNICATING WITH US.

On May 28, 1941, American Export Lines in Lisbon again confirmed the reservation of accommodations for the three Frühaufs on the *Exeter*, scheduled to sail on August 8, 1941 (Doc. 28). This booking would expire if the passengers did not report at the shipping line office at least four days prior to the sailing date of the ship.

DOCUMENT 28

American Export Lines, Inc.
25, Broadway, New York, U.S.A.
Agent
Joh. Beckmann
Lisbon

Lisbon, May 28th 1941

Mr. Felix Fruehauf
Augsburgerstrasse 37
Berlin W50

OUR REFERENCE: P.3495

Mr. Felix Fruehauf
Miss Helga Fruehauf
Master Rudolf Fruehauf

We confirm that, subject to the conditions of the Corporation's passage contract we have reserved the following accommodation for the above-mentioned person(s).
Steamer »EXETER«   Scheduled sailing Aug. 8th 1941
Accommodation guaranteed   Rate –

Such reservation will be cancelled unless the passenger calls at our office not less than four days before the above stated sailing date.

Very truly yours,
American Export Lines, Inc.,
(gez.) F. M. Citriolo.
Mgr. Pass. Dept.

Copy of an invoice for 532 marks from the forwarding firm
Schmiedecke in Berlin after the goods to be shipped had been
repacked into ten watertight wooden suitcase boxes (Doc. 29).
Another invoice from Schmiedecke for 7,350 marks covers air freight
charges from Berlin to Lisbon for 1,410 kilograms (3,113 pounds) of
baggage, including storage charges for two months (Doc. 30).
In a letter dated October 14, 1941, Felix Frühauf asked that Mr.
Schmiedecke refund the sum of 1,057.50 marks since the baggage
was not sent to Lisbon but only as far as Madrid (Doc. 31).

DOCUMENT 29

Abschrift   Berlin-Lankwitz, den 9. Mai 41
                                             Kiepertstraße 50

Hermann Schmiedecke
Transport–Verzollung
Spedition–Möbeltransport

Rechnung für Herrn Felix Israel Frühauf, Berlin

Umpackung, Verzollung, 2 Packer gestellt,
10 Kofferkisten mit Packungsmaterial geliefert,
und Malereiarbeiten ausgeführt   RM 532.–

Bitte den Betrag auf mein Bankkonto zu überweisen.

    gez. Hermann Schmiedecke

[Ich bitte obigen Betrag von RM 532.– Herrn Hermann Schmiedecke auf
dessen Bank-Konto zu überweisen zu Lasten meines Kontos 25 846.
z. Zt. Berlin W 50
Augsburgerstraße 37

                                    gez. Felix Israel Frühauf]

DOCUMENT 30

Abschrift   Berlin-Lankwitz, den 18. Mai 1941
                             Kiepertstraße 50

Hermann Schmiedecke
Transport–Verzollung
Spedition–Möbeltransport

Rechnung für Herrn Felix Israel Frühauf, Berlin

1410 kg Luftfracht von Berlin nach Lissabon
Expedition, Fuhrlohn von der Bahn zum Lager
Einlagern des Reisegepäcks 2 Monate Lagergeld,
Fuhrlohn vom Lager zum Lufthafen, u. s. w. lt.
Vereinbarung   RM 7 350.–
erhalten am 5. 4. 1941 von der
Verbandssparkasse Meiningen   RM 1 790,–
                                                      RM 5 560.–.

In diesem Betrag ist kein Kostenteil enthalten, der in
ausländischer Währung zu zahlen ist.
Bitte den Betrag auf m/ Konto bei der Deutschen Bank
zu überweisen.

                                    Hochachtungsvoll
                                    gez. Herm. Schmiedecke

[Ich bitte den Betrag zu Lasten m/ Kontos 25846 gefl. zu überweisen.
z. Zt. Bln. W 50
Augsburgerstraße 37   gez. Felix Israel Frühauf

Original-Rechnung befindet sich bei
der Verbandssparkasse.]

DOCUMENT 31

Felix Israel Frühauf   Berlin W 50, 14. 10. 1941
                                              Rankestr. 27ᵃ II

Abschrift

Herrn Herm. Schmiedecke
Spedition
Berlin-Lankwitz
Kiepertstraße 50.

Laut Rechnung vom 18. 5. 41 berechneten Sie mir:
1410 kg Luftfracht von Berlin nach Lissabon
   einschließlich aller Spesen   RM 7 350. –
Dagegen wurde das ges. Gepäck von Ihnen
nur bis Madrid zum Versand gebracht.
Es steht mir somit folgender Betrag zu:
Luftfracht Berlin–Lissabon per Kilo 4. 35
  "   " –Madrid " " <u>3.60</u>
             RM -.75

1410 kg a. 0.75 = <u>RM 1.057.50.</u>

Ich bitte um sofortige Überweisung auf mein Sicherungskonto 25846 bei der
Verbandssparkasse in Meiningen.

               Hochachtungsvoll
               gez. Felix Israel Frühauf.
Einschreiben!

Affidavits of Support made out by Meyer Vomberg (Doc. 32), who lived in Charlotte, Michigan, and his son Arthur J. Vomberg (Doc. 33), Felix Frühauf's uncle and cousin, respectively. The affidavits were dated April 19, 1941.

DOCUMENT 32 AND 33 FOLLOW

WMA-3274

4

United States of America
County of **Eaton**   } ss
State of **Michigan**

Affidavit of Support

    Myer Vomberg   residing at **221 E. Lovett St**
      (Name)   (Street Address)

   Charlotte   **Michigan**   being duly sworn depose and say:
    (City)   (State)

1. That I am a native born citizen of the | That I became a naturalized citizen of | That I declared my intention of becoming
United States having been born in the | the United States on: | a citizen of the United States on:

City of _____	Date **Oct 23, 1882** In	Date _____ In the
	Charlotte **Eaton**	(City) (County)
State of _____	(City) (County)	
	Michigan number	(State) number
	(State)	
	of my certificate being **No Number**	of my certificate being _____
	issued by the Court of **Circuit**	issued by the Court of _____
	Court of Eaton County	
	Michigan	

2. That it is my (our) intention and desire to have my (our) relatives whose names appear below, at present residing at:

    Meiningen, a.d Werra, Germany

(Give complete address)

come to the United States for permanent residence.

Name of Alien	Sex	Date of Birth	Country of Birth	Occupation	Relationship to Deponent
Felix Fruehauf	male	10-2-86	Germany	Merchant	Nephew
Rudolph Max Fruehauf	male		Germany	Son of Felix Fruehauf	
Helga Fruehauf	female		Germany	Daughter of Felix Fruehauf	

3. That my regular occupation is **Merchant—Farmer—Investor, The Vomberg Co**
                              (Business Name and Address)

    Charlotte, Michigan

and my average earnings amount to $ **3500.00 annually**

4. That I (We) possess the following financial assets of which corroborative evidence is herewith attached:

    Savings Account $5244.93   **Interest in The Vomberg Co**
    Life Insurance   8500.00   **$10300.00**
    Real Estate   19000.00
    Stocks and Bonds 32000.00

5. That my (our) dependents consist of **Wife)   Mary Vomberg**

That I (We) am (are) willing and able to receive, maintain, support the alien (s) after their immigration to the United States, and hereby assume such obligations guaranteeing that none of them will at any time become public charges upon any community in the United States; and that any of school age will be sent to school.

That this affidavit is made by me (us) voluntarily and of my (our) free will in order that our American Consul will issue visas to the above mentioned relatives so that they may enter the United States for permanent residence.

SWORN TO BEFORE ME THIS

    19   DAY OF *April*   19**41**   *Myer Vomberg*

Charles O. Rowe

Notary Public in and for Eaton County, Michigan

4449-3274

United States of America
County of __Eaton__
State of __Michigan__ } ss

Affidavit of Support

__Arthur J Vomberg__ residing at __321 E. Lovett St__
(Name) (Street Address)

__Charlotte__ __Michigan__ being duly sworn depose and say:
(City) (State)

1. That I am a native born citizen of the United States having been born in the | That I became a naturalized citizen of the United States on: | That I declared my intention of becoming a citizen of the United States on:

City of __Charlotte__

State of __Michigan__

	(City) (County)	(City) (County)
	(State) number	(State) number
	of my certificate being	of my certificate being
	issued by the Court of	issued by the Court of

Date ____ In ____ Date ____ In the ____

2. That it is my (our) intention and desire to have my (our) relatives whose names appear below, at present residing at:

__Meiningen, a d Werra, Germany__

(Give complete address)

come to the United States for permanent residence.

Name of Alien	Sex	Date of Birth	Country of Birth	Occupation	Relationship to Deponent
Felix Fruehauf	male	10-2-86	Germany	Merchant	Cousin
Rudolph Max Fruehauf	male		Germany		Son of Felix Fruehauf
Helga Fruehauf	female		Germany		Daughter of Felix Fruehauf

3. That my regular occupation is __Merchant---The Vomberg Co---Charlotte, Mich.__
(Business Name and Address)

and my average earnings amount to $ __2500.00 annually__

4. That I (We) possess the following financial assets of which corroborative evidence is herewith attached:

__Life Insurance $8000.00__

__Interest in The Vomberg Co $8100.00__

5. That my (our) dependents consist of __None__

That I (We) am (are) willing and able to receive, maintain, support the alien (s) after their immigration to the United States, and hereby assume such obligations guaranteeing that none of them will at any time become public charges upon any community in the United States; and that any of school age will be sent to school.

That this affidavit is made by me (us) voluntarily and of my (our) free will in order that our American Consul will issue visas to the above mentioned relatives so that they may enter the United States for permanent residence.

SWORN TO BEFORE ME THIS

Arthur J Vomberg

__19__ DAY OF __april__ 19__41__

Charles O. Roney

Notary Public in and for Eaton County, Michigan
P. O. Charlotte, Commission Expires July 5, '34   Form No. 93-3-41

A letter sent to Felix Frühauf by the Consular Section of the American Embassy in Berlin, dated May 7, 1941 (Doc. 34), asking him to appear on June 26, 1941, to make his formal visa application between 10 A.M. and 12 noon with all the documents required for his visa as listed on an enclosed memorandum (Doc. 35). The letter said the purpose of this formal visa application was "to establish whether you fulfill all the immigration laws of the United States."

DOCUMENT 34

811.11
HFC/nm

60119

AMERIKANISCHE BOTSCHAFT
Konsular-Abteilung

Berlin W.9, Datum d.Poststemp.
Hermann Goeringstr.21,

Herrn
Frau   *Fruhauf, Felise*
Fraeulein

Betr.: Ihre hier laufende Visumangelegenheit.

Es wird Ihnen von der Konsular-Abteilung der Amerikani-
schen Botschaft freigestellt, am

Juni 26. 1941

in der Zeit von 10 - 12 Uhr unter Vorlage der auf dem beilie-
genden Zettel "Zur Visumerteilung erforderliche Dokumente"
aufgezaehlten Papiere vorzusprechen und Ihren formellen Visum-
antrag zu stellen. Der Zweck eines formellen Visumantrages
ist der, festzustellen, ob Sie saemtlichen Einwanderungsgeset-
zen der Vereinigten Staaten genuegen.

Es liegt in Ihrem eigenen Interesse, keine definitiven
Vorbereitungen, wie z.B. Haushaltsaufloesung etc. zu treffen,
bevor Sie nicht im Besitze des Einwanderungsvisums sind.

Diese Einladung hat nur am genannten   Hochachtungsvoll
Tage Gueltigkeit, wenn Sie um-
gehend die von Ihnen geforderte   *HFCunningham*
genaue Passagebuchung einsenden.
Die von Ihnen am 21. April ds.Js.   H. Francis Cunningham, Jr.,
eingesandte Photokopie der Ame-   Amerikanischer Vizekonsul
rican Export Lines genuegt nicht
den hiesigen Anforderungen, weil
nicht daraus ersichtlich ist, ob
die Buchung tatsaechlich fest ist.

// ZUR BEACHTUNG ! //

Diese Einladung hat nur fuer den genannten
Tag Gueltigkeit und verfaellt, wenn sie
nicht eingehalten wird.

WARNUNG!
Die Erteilung eines Visums kann erst dann
erfolgen, wenn eine Quotenummer
verfügbar wird.

1 Anlage.

DOCUMENT 35

DIE ZUR VISUMERTEILUNG ERFORDERLICHEN DOKUMENTE.
-.-

1. Reisepass, gueltig fuer die Reise nach den Vereinigten Staaten
   (wenn nicht erhaeltlich, anderes gueltiges Reisedokument). Kinder duerfen im Pass der Eltern eingetragen sein, soweit dieses
   seitens der ausstellenden Behoerde zulaessig ist.
2. Pro Person drei gleiche, unaufgezogene Passbilder auf ganz duen-
   nem Papier, Format 4 ½ x 6 cm. Hintergrund einfarbig hell.
3. Standesamtliche Geburtsurkunde in doppelter Ausfuehrung pro Person (Geburtsschein, der nur ein Auszug aus dem Geburtenregister
   ist, genuegt nicht).
4. Standesamtliche Heiratsurkunde, wenn zutreffend; beglaubigte
   Abschrift des Scheidungsurteils, falls geschieden.
5. Standesamtliche Sterbeurkunde des Gatten bezw. der Gattin, wenn
   zutreffend.
6. Letzter polizeilicher Anmeldeschein (jetzigen Datums).
7. Polizeiliches Fuehrungszeugnis, in doppelter Ausfuehrung (fuer
   jede Person ueber 15 Jahre). Im Fuehrungszeugnis muessen saemtliche eventuell verhaengten Strafen verzeichnet sein, welche
   grundsaetzlich in Fuehrungszeugnissen aufgenommen werden, soweit
   sie im Strafregister verzeichnet sind und ungeachtet der Tatsa-
   che, wo und wann sie verhaengt worden sind. Aus den Fuehrungszeugnissen muss ebenfalls hervorgehen, wo die betreffende Person
   ab des 21. Lebensjahres gewohnt hat. Sollte dieses an verschiedenen Orten gewesen sein, dann ist es erforderlich, dass
   Fuehrungszeugnisse in doppelter Ausfertigung von jedem Ort bei-
   gebracht werden, in dem die betreffende Person waehrend dieses
   Zeitraumes wohnhaft war. (Es ist nochmals zu betonen, dass
   Fuehrungszeugnisse saemtliche verhaengten Strafen zu enthalten
   haben, auch solche, die mehr als fuenf Jahre zuruecklliegen !)
      // Sollte es unumgaenglich sein, Photokopien
         einzureichen, so werden diese nur anerkannt,
         wenn sie b e g l a u b i g t sind.   //
8. Pro Person Leumundszeugnisse von zwei verschiedenen Buergen
   in je dreifacher Ausfertigung. (Wenn moeglich, nicht von Ver-
   wandten). Die Unterschriften der Buergen auf den Leumundszeug-
   nissen muessen notariell beglaubigt sein.

Gebuehren : Antragstellung auf Einwanderungsvisum: $ 1,00 (ein
Dollar); Einwanderungsvisum: $ 9,00 (neun Dollar). Diese Gebuehren
sind von jedem Familienmitglied, also auch von Kindern, zu entrichten. Bereits entrichtete Gebuehren werden nicht zurueckerstattet,
selbst wenn das Visum unbenutzt bleibt oder verweigert wird.

Das Einwanderungsvisum hat eine maximale Gueltigkeitsdauer von
vier Monaten. Es kann n i c h t verlaengert werden.

Geburtsurkunden und Fuehrungszeugnisse werden dem Einwanderer nicht
zurueckgegeben. Bei Verweigerung des Visums wird je ein Exemplar
dieser Dokumente zurueckerstattet.

          LETZTES FUEHRUNGSZEUGNIS MUSS NEUESTEN DATUMS
          SEIN, KEINESFALLS AELTER ALS 4 WOCHEN VOR-
                    LADUNGSTERMIN.

              -.-.-.-.-.-.-.-.-.-.-

Receipt showing that Felix Frühauf had handed over his savings
account book number 25,846, containing 17,226.09 marks, to the
savings bank in Meiningen, the Verbandssparkasse Meiningen-Zella-
Mehlis (Doc. 36).

DOCUMENT 36

Empfangsbescheinigung

Herrn
Felix Frühauf
Meiningen

Betr. **Sparbuch Nr.** 25846 *der Verbandssparkasse Meiningen – Zella-Mehlis*

Gläubiger: Felix Frühauf, Meiningen
Derzeitiges Guthaben RM: 17.226.09

Obiges Sparbuch empfingen wir von Ihnen zur Aufbewahrung.
Die Aushändigung des Sparbuches erfolgt an jeden Inhaber dieser Empfangsbescheinigung gegen deren Rückgabe (§ 808 BGB). Die Sparkasse ist berech-
tigt, aber nicht verpflichtet, die Legitimation des Abholers zu prüfen.
Die Empfangsbescheinigung ist daher sorgfältig aufzubewahren.

Meiningen, den 15. März 1941.

Heil Hitler!
Verbandssparkasse
Meiningen – Zella-Mehlis
gez. Groß

On May 11, 1941, Felix Frühauf applied to the Regional Office of the
Finance Ministry in Rudolstadt for an increase of 150 marks in his
allowance (it had been set at 410 marks) because the cost of living in
Berlin was higher than in Meiningen (Doc. 37). Instead of raising his
allowance, the regional office notified him on February 13, 1942, that
it had been reduced to 250 marks (Doc. 38). The reasons for this
reduction are not clear. Perhaps it was a form of harassment because
the authorities had found out that Felix Frühauf had been living in
Berlin since the start of 1941 and that he had subsequently moved
twice without reporting the change of address as required. In addition, he had been asked repeatedly, under threat of punishment, to
inform, in writing, all those who owed him money that any moneys
owed to him must be paid into his blocked account. Copies of these
letters were to be deposited with the foreign exchange office. Furthermore, for two years, in spite of repeated requests to do so, he had
not named his mother-in-law Lina Schwerin's heirs (Doc. 39).

DOCUMENT 37

Felix Israel Frühauf   Berlin W.50, den 11. Mai 1941
                                            Augsburgerstrasse 37 bei Werres

An den
Herrn Oberfinanzpräsidenten
Thüringen (Devisenstelle)
Rudolstadt

Betrifft: Sicherungsanordnung vom 9. 9. 39 und 29. 9. 39
          Geschäftszeichen JS 114 Sch/L.

Laut Bescheid vom 29. September 1939 ist mir ein Betrag von RM 410.– pro
Monat freigestellt worden.
Ich wohne mit meinen beiden Kindern zur Zeit in Berlin und bitte ich den
Herrn Oberfinanzpräsidenten die Freigrenze pro Monat um RM 150.– zu er-
höhen, da der Lebensunterhalt in Berlin höher als in Meiningen ist.

                                            gez. Felix Israel Frühauf
                                            Kennkarte J. Meiningen
                                            Nr. A 00381

DOCUMENT 38

**Der Oberfinanzpräsident
Thüringen**
(Devifenstelle)

Rudolstadt, 13. Febr. 1942
Straße der SA. 60
Fernruf 524

Geschäftszeichen: J S 114 IV Geißler

An

Einschreiben

Herrn

z. Hd. de Felix Israel Frühauf

Meiningen (Thür.) *[handwritten]*

[handwritten]

[handwritten]

Anl.: 1. Abschr.

Den im Abschn. I Ziff. 3 meiner Sicherungsanordnung vom

9.9.1939 Gesch.-Z. J S 114 Sch/Pa vorgesehenen

Freibetrag setze ich mit Wirkung vom 1. dieses Monats auf

RM 250.-- (i. B. RM zweihundertfünfzig)

je Kalendermonat fest.

hat erhalten.
Abschrift dieses Bescheids für die kontoführende Bank liegt bei.

Im Auftrag

[signature]

Vordr. Dev. VI 3 Nr. 4 **(K 326)**

28. 8. 39. 3000
DW 476 A 5

DOCUMENT 39

Der Oberfinanzpräsident Thüringen
- Devisenstelle -

Rudolfstadt, 5.Oktober 1942
Straße der SA. 60
Fernsprecher: Sammelnummer 524
Sprechzeit: nur 9—13 Uhr

Geb./ JS 354 IV Bock
(Bitte in jeder Zuschrift angeben)

Mit Postzustellungsurkunde
Herrn
Felix Israel Frühauf

Berlin W 50
Rankestr.27 A II

Betreff
Sicherungsanordnung gegen die verstorbene Jüdin
Lina Sara Schwerin, Meiningen, Straße der SA 18

Ich beziehe mich nochmals auf die mit meinem
Schreiben vom 12.5.42 übersandte Abschrift meines
Schreibens an Sie vom 19.3.42 sowie auf Ihr
Schreiben vom 14.5.42 und ersuche nochmals um
umgehende Mitteilung, ob die Erben der verstorbenen Lina Sara Schwerin nunmehr feststehen. Beja-
hendenfalls wollen Sie Abs.4 meines Schreibens
an Sie vom 19.3.42 umgehend beantworten.

Im Auftrage

In a letter dated November 12, 1952, the Jewish Restitution Successor Organization in Berlin stated that Felix Frühauf and his son had been transported to an unknown destination on February 19, 1943, with the Twenty-ninth Eastern Transport (*Osttransport*) (Doc. 40). A letter from the Berlin Jewish Community dated November 17, 1952, contained the same information (Doc. 41).

The International Tracing Service of the Red Cross in Arolsen, Germany, after laborious research, discovered that the names Felix and Rudolf Frühauf did not appear on the transport list of the Berlin Gestapo for February 19, 1943 (the Twenty-ninth Eastern Transport [*Osttransport*], but that they did appear on the list of those deported to Auschwitz on August 24, 1943 (Doc. 42).

According to the Frankfurt am Main police transport list, Felix Frühauf was transferred from the police prison in Frankfurt am Main to Berlin on August 2, 1943 (Doc. 43).

A Decision of the District Court of Berlin-Charlottenburg of July 6, 1961, officially declared that the deaths of Felix Frühauf and Rudolf Max Frühauf had occurred on May 8, 1945, the day the war ended (Doc. 44).

DOCUMENT 40

Jewish Restitution Successor Organization
Berlin Regional Office
Berlin-Dahlem

Berlin, den 12. November 1952

Herrn
Dr. Walter Stephan
Berlin W 30.

Motzstr. 5

Betr.: FRUEHAUF, Felix, geb. 2. 10. 1886 Walldorf
       FRUEHAUF, Rudolf, geb. 6. 11. 1922 Meiningen
       letzte Anschrift: Berlin W., Rankestr. 27 a

Auf Ihre Anfrage nach den Obengenannten teilen wir Ihnen mit, dass laut der
uns vorliegenden Deportationskartei die Betreffenden

43/25153   mit dem 29. Osttransport am 19. 2. 1943
               nach unbekannt

deportiert wurden.

Hochachtungsvoll
Stempel   gez. i. A. Eisner
                                           JRSO Berlin Regional Office

DOCUMENT 41

Jüdische Gemeinde zu Berlin
Allgemeine Verwaltung
Hauptverwaltung

Berlin N 4, den 17. November 1952
Oranienburger Straße 28

Helga B a d e r, Frankfurt-Rödelheim (M.)
Reichsburgstr. 4

Betrifft: Felix F r ü h a u f, geb. 2. X. 86 in Walldorf.
zuletzt wohnhaft gewesen in Berlin W. 50., Rankestraße. 27 a / Sommerfeld.

Unseren Ermittlungen zufolge ist der Obengenannte
mit dem   29. Ost   -Transport am 19. 2. 1943
nach   deportiert worden.
Der Obengenannte hat sich bis zum heutigen Tage hier nicht zurückgemeldet.
Wir bedauern sehr, Ihnen einen günstigeren Bescheid nicht geben zu können.

Hochachtungsvoll
Stempel   gez. Unterschrift

DOCUMENT 42 FOLLOWS

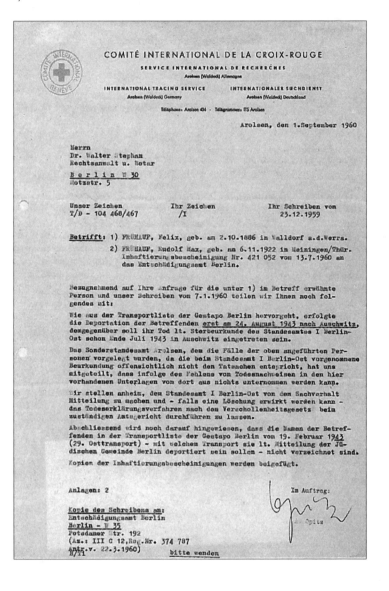

COMITÉ INTERNATIONAL DE LA CROIX-ROUGE

SERVICE INTERNATIONAL DE RECHERCHES
Arolsen (Waldeck) Allemagne

INTERNATIONAL TRACING SERVICE   INTERNATIONALER SUCHDIENST
Arolsen (Waldeck) Germany   Arolsen (Waldeck) Deutschland

Téléphone: Arolsen 434 - Télégrammes: ITS Arolsen

Arolsen, den 1.September 1960

Herrn
Dr. Walter Stephan
Rechtsanwalt u. Notar
B e r l i n W 30
Motzstr. 5

Unser Zeichen   Ihr Zeichen   Ihr Schreiben von
T/D - 104 468/467   /I   23.12.1959

Betrifft: 1) FRÜHAUF, Felix, geb. am 2.10.1886 in Walldorf a.d.Werra.

          2) FRÜHAUF, Rudolf Max, geb. am 6.11.1922 in Meiningen/Thür.
             Inhaftierungsbescheinigung Nr. 421 052 vom 13.7.1960 an
             das Entschädigungsamt Berlin.

Bezugnehmend auf Ihre Anfrage für die unter 1) im Betreff erwähnte
Person und unser Schreiben vom 7.1.1960 teilen wir Ihnen noch folgendes mit:

Wie aus der Transportliste der Gestapo Berlin hervorgeht, erfolgte
die Deportation der Betreffenden erst am 24. August 1943 nach Auschwitz,
demgegenüber soll ihr Tod lt. Sterbeurkunde des Standesamtes I Berlin-
Ost schon Ende Juli 1943 in Auschwitz eingetreten sein.

Das Sonderstandesamt Arolsen, dem die Fälle der oben angeführten Personen vorgelegt wurden, da die beim Standesamt I Berlin-Ost vorgenommene
Beurkundung offensichtlich nicht den Tatsachen entspricht, hat uns
mitgeteilt, dass infolge des Fehlens von Todesnachweisen in den hier
vorhandenen Unterlagen von dort aus nichts unternommen werden kann.

Wir stellen anheim, dem Standesamt I Berlin-Ost von dem Sachverhalt
Mitteilung zu machen und - falls eine Löschung erwirkt werden kann -
das Todeserklärungsverfahren nach dem Verschollenheitsgesetz beim
zuständigen Amtsgericht durchführen zu lassen.

Abschliessend wird noch darauf hingewiesen, dass die Namen der Betreffenden in der Transportliste der Gestapo Berlin vom 19. Februar 1943
(29. Osttransport) - mit welchem Transport sie lt. Mitteilung der Jüdischen Gemeinde Berlin deportiert sein sollen - nicht verzeichnet sind.
Kopien der Inhaftierungsbescheinigungen werden beigefügt.

Anlagen: 2   Im Auftrag:

Kopie des Schreibens an:
Entschädigungsamt Berlin
Berlin - W 35
Potsdamer Str. 192   Opitz
(Az.: III C 12,Reg.Nr. 374 787
Antr.v. 22.3.1960)   bitte wenden

Kopie des Schreibens an:
Frau Helga Cohn
Frankfurt/M.-Süd
Schadowstr. 5

(Ihr Schrb.v. 21.6.1960)

DOCUMENT 43

Comité International de La Croix-Rouge
Service International de Recherches
Arolsen (Waldeck) Allemagne

Arolsen, den 13. Juli 1960

Frau   *Eingangsstempel v. 29. 9. 1960*
Helga Cohn

FRANKFURT/M.-Süd
Schadowstr. 5

Betrifft: FRÜHAUF, Felix, geboren am 2. 10. 1886 in Walldorf a. d. Werra.

Sehr geehrte Frau Cohn!
In der Anlage übersenden wir Ihnen eine Informationskopie der hier vorbereiteten Bescheinigung für die obengenannte Person. [...]
In unseren Unterlagen ist noch folgende Information vorhanden:
FRÜHAUF, Felix., Gef.Nr. 4871, wurde am 2. August 1943 vom
Polizeigefängnis Frankfurt/Main nach Berlin überstellt.
Geprüfte Unterlagen: Transportliste der Polizeibehörden Frankfurt/Main.
Infolge der unvollständigen Personalangaben können wir nicht feststellen, ob
dieser Bericht auf die obengenannte Person zutrifft.

Anlage: Hochachtungsvoll
1 Informationskopie   Im Auftrag:
d. Inhaft.Beschein.   Für die Richtigkeit:
                                        gez. A. Opitz

DOCUMENT 44

Beglaubigte Abschrift
Beschluss
Der Tod folgender Personen wird mit Zeitpunkt
8. Mai 1945 festgestellt:

1) Kaufmann Felix Frühauf,
geboren am 2. 10. 1886 in Walldorf/Werra,

2) Gerber Rudolf Max Frühauf,
geboren am 6. 11. 1922 in Meiningen/Thür.,

beide zuletzt wohnhaft gewesen in
Berlin W 50, Rankestr. 27 a bei Sommerfeld.
Diese Entscheidung ergeht gebührenfrei, die notwendigen Auslagen trägt der Nachlass.
Gründe.
Die Genannten wurden durch den 41. Osttransport der Gestapo Berlin am 24. 8. 1943 nach dem Vernichtungslager Auschwitz verschleppt und sind seitdem spurlos verschwunden. Unter diesen Umständen ist ihr Tod durch Ausrottungsmassnahmen nicht zu bezweifeln. Die beantragten Ermittlungen nach den genauen Todesdaten sind erfolglos geblieben. Als wahrscheinlichster Todeszeitpunkt kann daher nur der 8. Mai 1945 als Tag des Kriegsendes festgestellt werden.
Dieser Beschluss beruht auf §§ 1 (Abs. 2), 39 ff. VerschG, Art. 2 Versch-ÄndG. Er widerlegt die Sterbeurkunden Nr. 6781/1949 und 6779/1949 des Standesamts I Berlin vom 18. 6. 1949, in denen unrichtigerweise die Todeszeit beider Vermissten mit Ende Juli 1943 angenommen ist.
Berlin-Charlottenburg, den 19. April 1961
Amtsgericht Charlottenburg, Abteilung 70
Fest, Amtsgerichtsrat
Ausgefertigt:
L.S. gez. Baum
Justizangestellte (Baum)
als Urkundsbeamter der Geschäftsstelle des
Amtsgerichts Charlottenburg.
Vorstehender Beschluss ist seit dem 27. Juni 1961 rechtskräftig.
Berlin-Charlottenburg, den 6. Juli 1961
L.S. gez. Unterschrift, Justizoberinspektor
als Urkundsbeamter der Geschäftsstelle des Amtsgerichts

Beglaubigt zwecks Zustellung
Der Rechtsanwalt
gez. Unterschrift